Soviet Strategy for Economic Growth

INDIANA UNIVERSITY

INTERNATIONAL STUDIES

NICOLAS SPULBER

Soviet Strategy for Economic Growth

INDIANA UNIVERSITY PRESS
Bloomington & London

This book is published in cooperation with the Russian and East European Institute of Indiana University.

A companion volume, *Foundations of Soviet Strategy for Economic Growth: Selected Soviet Essays, 1924-1930*, edited by Nicolas Spulber, published simultaneously by Indiana University Press, contains translations of the more important Soviet articles on which the present study is based.

Preface

AN ECONOMIC plan is both a final result and a beginning. It is the product of compromises among competing goals; the reflection of a basic strategy of how best to allocate resources in order to reach these goals; and the embodiment of certain principles of planning and methods of implementing them. It is, on the other hand, a program of action, combining directives with forecasts concerning investment, output, and employment, and intended to expand a country's productive capacity and to bring about a new pattern of interdependence between sectors of the economy.

The choice of a strategy of development and the determination of principles and methods of planning were heatedly debated in the Soviet Union on the eve of its era of forced industrialization and comprehensive planning, which began in 1929. During these debates the Soviets grappled with some of the disconcerting problems and crucial difficulties which today confront the policy makers of underdeveloped areas, who wish to industrialize their countries rapidly.

While the Russians had greatly modified their institutional

setting, and while they believed that in this manner they could sweep away many of their basic economic problems, they soon discovered that their expectations were harshly contradicted by facts. Changes in institutional arrangements, no matter how deep, do not *per se* modify the complex dependence of a small domestic industrial sector upon the output, employment, savings, investment, and rate of growth of the overwhelming agricultural sector. They do not simplify the task of the policy maker and planner who wishes to launch his country on the path of industrialization and who needs for this purpose to select realistically among alternative patterns and paces of development. They do not guide his technological options, and they do not help him to decide where and how to start his "planning." Nor do they finally solve the typical problems of backwardness: the unresponsiveness of the price mechanism, the poorness or lack of economic information, the acute scarcity of labor skills. Hence the Soviet debates of the mid-1920's on strategies of development, pace of growth and efficiency, planning theory and practice clarify not only the underlying concepts and assumptions of the Soviet strategy of industrialization and Soviet planning, but also some of the basic problems of economic development in general.

During Stalin's "monolithic" rule the nature and content of the debates of the mid-1920's were systematically falsified. Many of the debaters themselves—V. G. Groman, V. A. Bazarov, N. I. Bukharin, E. A. Preobrazhenskii, and others—were "liquidated" with or without fictitious trials during the 1930's, their memory was vilified and their ideas distorted beyond recognition. The Soviet Union under Khrushchev has tried since the mid-1950's to disentangle itself somewhat from Stalin's bloody heritage. It has connected some of its present policies to solutions advanced in the 1920's, and has "rehabilitated" selectively, *post mortem,* some of the debaters. In so doing it has come to realize, in the economic field, the significance of some of the alternatives sacrificed in the 1920's—concerning, for instance, efficiency, consistency, and optimality in planning. Having discovered of late the pioneering attempts in input-output analysis of P. I. Popov, L. N. Litoshenko, and M. Barengol'ts, the Soviet bureaucracy which yesterday crushed these men is ready today to stake the wildest claims for "its" intellectual pioneers.

What is the validity of such claims? What is the actual content of the debates of the mid-1920's and to what extent do the concepts and assumptions of that period determine current Soviet thought on growth and planning? To what extent have these assumptions been revised through Soviet practice, modified, adjusted, and adapted to other purposes than those originally contemplated? Which specific problems, dilemmas, and solutions of the 1920's illumine the present-day problems and choices of the policy makers of the underdeveloped areas?

To clarify these questions, the present book examines the Soviet (1) goals and concepts of economic development; (2) views of the economy as a "going concern;" (3) strategies for carrying out these goals; (4) concepts of growth and efficiency; and (5) planning solutions—as formulated on the eve of the Soviet era of "all-out" industrialization and comprehensive planning and as modified since then. In a companion volume entitled *Foundations of Soviet Strat-*

egy for Economic Growth I present a broad selection of
Soviet economic essays of 1924-1930, revealing the whole
spectrum of the solutions proposed in respect to strategy and
planning on the eve of the era of all-out industrialization.
The two books thus present both an integrated view of the
economic debates of the Soviet 1920's, and a detailed view of
the "building blocks" of Soviet thought in respect to economic development. A bibliography included in the present
volume lists Soviet and non-Soviet sources concerning the
problems of rapid growth and the specific Soviet strategy
and planning methods. An extensively annotated bibliography included in the companion volume guides the reader
to the abundant Soviet materials concerning each of the various economic debates of the Soviet mid-1920's.

I am deeply indebted to all those who have helped me to
complete this work, which spanned a number of years. It is
a pleasure to acknowledge my great indebtedness to Professor Philip E. Mosely for helpful advice during the early
phase of this project and to Professors John P. Lewis and
Louis Shere of Indiana University, who read the first draft
of the present work and made numerous and extremely val-
uable suggestions. I am also very grateful to Mrs. Constance
R. Pitchell for editing the original draft, and to Miss Miriam
S. Farley of Indiana University Press for the preparation of
the final draft for publication; both have immeasurably im-
proved the readability of the text. I thank Mr. Arthur W.
Wright for preparing the index. I am further indebted to
the Ford Foundation, the American Council of Learned
Societies and its Joint Slavic and East European Grants
Committee, and to the Graduate Faculty of Indiana Univer-

sity, whose material help rendered this work possible. Of course, neither the persons nor the institutions who have helped me bear any responsibility for the content of this work.

NICOLAS SPULBER

Bloomington, Indiana

Contents

Soviet Strategy for Economic Growth

1 Goals and Instruments of Economic Development

W HAT is economic development or underdevelopment? The question is complex and elusive. The customary yardstick of a country's level of development is its per capita product. This yardstick subsumes in fact a number of interrelated indicators which define the specific economic, demographic, and technological characteristics of a given country at a given period of its history. When translated into some international unit, the per capita product enables us to see the position of each country in relation to other countries on a world scale. Growth in total and per capita product may occur without leading to a shift in rank on the world's per capita product scales; such a shift depends not only on the nature and extent of the changes which occur in a given country's capacity to produce goods, but also on the changes which occur simultaneously in all other countries.

Changes in a country's economic performance may be deliberately sought on the basis of a highly individualized type of policy tailored to the specific needs of any given underdeveloped country. Individualized policies may aim to achieve, over a selected time period, "adequate" per capita food supplies, clothing, and shelter, a more "equitable" land distribution, a more "satisfactory" taxation system, or any similar goal. In each case what would be considered adequate, equitable, or satisfactory would vary. What would be considered as appropriate minimum clothing and housing in the tropics would differ from the acceptable minimum in Labrador. Assuming that an underdeveloped country lacked a sufficiently responsive market mechanism, it would be the task of its policy makers and planners to define the "appropriate" goals and to gear the economy to meet them. This type of action would lead in time to genuine development, even though the country's relative rank on the world scale might remain the same. In our rapidly changing world, as in *Through the Looking-Glass*, it may take a lot of running to stay in the same (relative) place.

The betterment of a country's rank on the world scale involves a different type of goals and of means. The lag between a slowly developing country operating under an individualized type of policy and the leading countries using on an ever increasing scale the rapidly evolving technology of our time is increasingly difficult to bridge. The lag may be dramatically accented even when there are no severe disparities in resources between advancing and lagging countries. If one thinks of the relative position on the world per capita income scale of, say, Russia in the 1920's, or Brazil in the 1960's, one will realize how crucial it is to lag in technology. The head start of a leading country may have resulted from a unique combination of political, economic, demographic, cultural, and psychological elements; but the maintenance of this advance is secured not only through efficient use of resources under prevailing scarcities and unchanged technology, but above all through the continuous introduction of rapidly evolving techniques.

Changes in techniques imply not only changes in ways of using a fixed budget of resources but also changes in the size and composition of this budget itself. The policy maker of a newly developing country, if he aims to shift the relative position of his country on the world per capita product scale, can hardly satisfy himself with an "individualized" policy drawn, as it were, independently of the level of technology prevailing in the advanced countries. He must, on the contrary, take into account prevailing techniques and their prospective changes in the leading countries, ways of transplanting these techniques massively and adjusting them rapidly to his own country's conditions. Liquidation of underdevelopment may thus be looked upon not only as achieving sustained growth in per capita product but also as a race to close a growing technological gap—between various sectors within each country and between different countries.[1] Such a conception of development involves, however, not independent, entirely individualized marginal policies, but massive changes in technology.

The crux of the matter is that the smaller and less well endowed a country is, and the lower it is on the world per capita product scale, then the more massive, other things being equal, its technological shift must be. The crucial problems which the policy makers of the emerging nations face in this respect are how to span in practice—in isolation or if possible in conjunction with other countries joined in some supranational association—an already immense and ever increasing technological gap, how to secure the massive investments which such changes entail, how to order among themselves the various possible and "necessary" branch and sectoral projects, and finally how to select among competing processés the combination able to yield both the largest total and the most appropriate product mix.

The Soviet debates carried out between 1924 and 1930, during the preparation of an all-out industrialization drive and of an all-embracing planning system, are of crucial interest in these respects. Notwithstanding the specific framework within which these debates occurred, the peculiarities of the instruments used for achieving the Soviet policy makers' goals, and the misconceptions on which these policy makers operated, the Soviet experience is as revealing in its preparation as it is in its results.

Let us first recall that the Soviet policy makers' concepts about the scope and the possible and "necessary" pace of industrialization of their country changed rapidly during the early 1920's. The XIIth Party Congress and the XIIIth Party Conference, held respectively in April 1923 and January 1924, affirmed that "only a fundamental change in the political and economic situation in the industrial countries of Europe could seriously weaken the direct dependence of state industry on the position of peasant agriculture and create the conditions for a most rapid passage to the socialist economy."[2] In other words, only the spread of the Communist revolution to the industrialized countries of Europe could create conditions favorable for the industrialization of Russia and its rapid passage to a socialist economy; only this could free Russian industry from its direct dependence on the output and capacity to save of Russian agriculture. But when the prospect of immediate foreign revolutions disap-

peared, the XIVth Congress, held in December 1925, decided to stress that Russia itself had, after all, everything
that was necessary to construct in isolation a "fully socialist
society," and that the major goal of the Russian Communist
Party was precisely to build "full socialism" in a "single
country," the USSR.[3]

In Marxian theory one economic system supersedes another because its productivity is higher.[4] Capitalist productivity exceeded by far the productivity of the feudal com-
munity. Full socialism, according to this theory, should far
exceed the productivity of capitalism. By setting the goal
of constructing full socialism in the USSR the Soviet leaders
implied, and soon affirmed, that their aim was to increase
both the productive capacity of the country and its productivity to the point where they would "catch up with, in a
minimal historical period, and then surpass the level of
industrial development in the advanced capitalist countries,"[5] through the means and efforts of an immense but
backward, badly shattered, and isolated country. The Soviet
goal of economic development was defined as a massive
shift in rank on the world's per capita product scale in the
shortest possible period.

To place in perspective the magnitude of the shift involved in this goal, it is interesting to recall that in the late
twenties Soviet per capita income may be estimated (in
1954 prices) at some $285 against $1,510 for the United
States, that is, at 18.8 per cent or less than one-fifth of the
latter.[6] The Soviet Union's relative position in the mid-
1920's was similar to that of Brazil in the mid-1950's, and
much higher than that of China or India.

In the 1920's the USSR, with a population and a territory

roughly two and a half times as large as that of Brazil,[7] had 80 per cent of its working population in agriculture and 20 per cent in nonfarm occupations, against 65 per cent and 35 per cent for Brazil in the 1950's. The ratio of industrial personnel to total population stood, however, in both countries in these two periods at 2.5 per cent. Except for certain key industries such as steel and metal-working, and some large agricultural developments, both countries relied essentially on backward or even primitive techniques in small-scale industry, handicrafts, and small-scale peasant farming. The technological characteristics of underdeveloped countries which were typical of both Russia and Brazil—poor technology, low amount of power per worker employed, low output per worker—were accompanied by the equally familiar demographic and cultural characteristics of underdevelopment: high fertility and mortality rates, dietary deficiencies in large segments of the population, rudimentary hygiene, high illiteracy.

In terms of income structure, agriculture in the USSR contributed up to 38 per cent of the total in the mid-1920's, against 30 per cent in Brazil in the mid-1950's, and industry and construction contributed 31 per cent against 23 per cent in Brazil. The per capita outputs of some key commodities were similar in the two countries: the USSR produced in the mid-twenties 10 kilograms of pig iron against 18 in Brazil and 14 kilograms of steel against 19 in Brazil. If in relative terms the USSR stood higher than Brazil on the world scale for various crucial commodities, still a vast gulf separated it from the U.S. economy. In the mid-twenties Russia produced 1.5 per cent of the world's coal output, 2.0 per cent of its iron, 2.4 per cent of its steel, and 2.4 per cent of its electricity—against 45.0, 48.7, 51.8, and 43.2 per cent respectively for the United States. Brazil produced in the mid-fifties only 0.1, 0.5, 0.4, and 0.9 per cent, respectively, of world output in these branches; but the technology to which it now has access is far more advanced and versatile than that available to the Soviets in the 1920's.

The problems faced by the Soviet policy makers in the twenties offer in certain respects close analogies to those faced today by low-income areas. The Soviet policy makers' goal of expanding the country's productive capacity, of raising its productivity, and of increasing sharply the level of per capita income recognized the need, now familiar in many underdeveloped areas, to cut through the vicious circle of low total income, low savings, and slow growth, and to secure at the same time revolutionary technological changes in certain branches of the economy. But the central goal of "catching up with" and even "surpassing" the most advanced countries was in the case of the USSR tied to a number of other aims—(a) the construction of an advanced industrial and military establishment, and (b) the liquidation in the process of industrialization of all "pre-capitalist and capitalist forms of production," particularly in small industry, handicrafts, and agriculture. The aim of constructing an unsurpassed military establishment stemmed from the assumption that the Soviet system was engaged in a combat to the finish with the outside capitalist world. The aim of liquidating all other types of production and distribution within the USSR stemmed from the assumption that free-enterprise relationships, even in secondary sectors, engender forces hostile to the Soviet regime. The liquidation of "primitive" economic forms was taken to mean both the liquidation of certain social classes in the USSR—notably rich peasants and merchants—and the systematic elimination of market relationships in the economy as a whole, as we shall see subsequently.

The Soviet policy makers achieved from the onset of their regime an enormous concentration of power. All political power and a large share of economic power were concentrated in the leadership of the Communist party and the Soviet state. The nationalization of very large proportions of the key economic sectors (particularly industry, banking, trade, and transport) placed under the guidance and control of the party the "commanding heights" of the economy. It soon appeared, however, that the centralized management of the economy as a whole raised a number of problems completely distinct from the question of the extent of nationalization. In his speech at the last party congress he attended in 1922, Lenin remarked: "Here we have lived a year with the state in our hands, and under the New Economic Policy has it operated our way? No. We don't like to acknowledge this, but it hasn't. And how has it operated? The machine isn't going where we guide it, but where some illegal, or lawless, or God-knows-whence-derived speculators or private capitalistic businessmen, either the one or the other, are guiding it. A machine doesn't always travel just exactly the way, and it often travels just exactly not the way, that the man imagines who sits at the wheel."[8]

Some believed that it would be enough to liquidate the "Nepmen and the kulaks"—the new merchants and the rich peasants—and to establish an all-embracing central plan in order to have the machine "travel just exactly the way" the Central Committee of the Party wanted it to. Others pointed out that all-round planning, in order to "supplant the anarchy" of market-directed relationships and avoid severe inter-sector disproportions, depression, and waste, required (a) a clear understanding of the ways in which the Soviet economy was already solving the problems of how, what, and for whom to produce; (b) a clearly thought through policy of allocating the bulk of investments; (c) some guiding lines as to what was actually feasible in terms of growth and some broad rules as to how to allocate resources throughout the economy among alternative branches likely to yield similar outputs, among alternative processes, or between present and future outlays; (d) a good understanding of how to reach consistency between goals as well as between decisions taken at the top and their implementation at the bottom.

Those who thought that the "liquidation" of the Nepmen and of the kulaks would solve everything looked with suspicion and even open distrust on some of the discussions which started to develop among the country's economists. Those who understood that the centralized management of a single multi-branch, multi-plant corporation called the USSR poses an enormously complex and vital set of problems for the regime—concerning the conceptual system of the economy itself, the strategy of allocating investments, the rate of growth to be selected, and the planning procedure to be followed—engaged with violence and passion in the debates, which, unfortunately, marred and obscured some lines of the argument involved.

The debates, however, reached great depth, thanks to the appreciable intellectual freedom of the Soviet mid-twenties, the personal participation in the discussion of many non-

Communist specialists who had rallied to the regime—mostly Social Democrats, Populists, or apolitical specialists—the lack of absolute centralization or rigid coordination among economic agencies and ministries, and finally the deep split among party factions before the establishment of the rule of an absolutely monolithic party obeying the inspired voice of an infallible chief. The canvass of the twenties was dominated by a large and varied number of personalities, agencies, and journals.

2 The Soviet Economy and Economic Laws

THE formulation of a well-grounded policy of economic development requires both properly systematized knowledge about factor endowments and their utilization (i.e., co-ordinated information about relations of inputs to outputs, sectoral interdependence, and uses of the final product) and some guiding principles as to the mechanisms by which that economy determines what, how, and for whom to produce. Paradoxically, the Soviet policy makers engaged in the mid-1920's in the formulation of their long-range policy of economic development and of their strategy for concentrating investible resources before they had secured either fully satisfactory information about their economy or a clear-cut understanding of its working principles.

In order to understand both this paradox and the frame of reference in which this long-range policy was formulated, one must understand some of the basic assumptions of Marxian economic theory and the ways in which its application was viewed as relevant in the Soviet economy of the 1920's. In Marxian theory, production relations and property relations are determined jointly by the level of development of the society's material forces of production, that is, by the nature and development of its labor force and of its technology. Production relations and property relations correspond "to the *stage* of development of [society's] material powers of production,"[1] as Marx puts it. The *mode* of production determines in fact not only the economic structure of the society, but also "the general character of the social, political, and spiritual processes of life."[2] When dealing with broad historical economic changes, Marx always focuses on changes in the mode of production and not on any other changes in "economic factors," as is usually and erroneously assumed. Further, Marx is always concerned with changing social relations, what he calls "relationships among classes," and not with individual reactions to a given social environment. Finally, for Marx each economic problem is shaped by the given historic and social setting in which it appears. Each problem is tied to a given setting and the economic principles evolved from its study are assumed to have only a transient, historically limited application. Principles, or integrated theories—called in Marxian terminology "laws," as in the natural sciences[3]—are deemed to hold sway only within given socio-historical limits. In other words, Marxism postulates (a) priority of production methods over all other economic or para-economic factors for determining the characteristics of any society; (b) priority of social phenomena over any individual actions, desires, or tastes; and (c) transience of all economic "laws" (principles).[4]

Within this general framework, two distinct schools of thought emerged in the 1920's among Soviet policy makers, planners, and economists. This basic division, which has manifested itself under a variety of forms since then, has never in fact been bridged by arguments fully consistent with the rest of the Marxist theory and equally acceptable to both groups. The first of these schools stressed the importance of the conscious, voluntary element in the construction of socialism, namely, the importance of the role of the party and of the policies it freely determines. The second school stressed the existence of certain "laws" or of empirically observable "regularities," objective constraints which limit the sphere of the party's intervention and may often thwart its decisions. The "voluntarists" were split as to the specific policies or general strategy of development which the party should lay down and follow throughout the transition period from capitalism to socialism. The "determinists"—partisans of the necessity to recognize and conform to objective "laws"[5]—were for their part divided as to the exact impact of this or that general "law," or this or that constraint on the policy of the party. The dichotomy voluntarism-determinism is clearly apparent in the Soviet approaches to the economics of socialism, to the Soviet strategy of economic development, and to Soviet planning theory and practice.[6]

In the field of economic theory, the camp of the "voluntarists" was led at the beginning of the 1920's by N. I. Bukharin and E. A. Preobrazhenskii, two outstanding Soviet policy makers and economists who later clashed violently on the question of what specific policies the party should follow on the road to communism. Bukharin and Preobrazhenskii—coauthors of a famous party manual on economics[7]—contended that economics as developed by Marx studies only the operation of market-directed commodity-producing societies. Under communism, so the argument of this school runs, economics and its "categories"—money, prices, wages, interest, rent, profits—disappear, giving place to direct material ac-

counting. Over-all planning, viewed as a system of organization directly opposed to the market process, would supplant
the latter entirely. "Commodities" (goods sold and bought
by different owners), which are typical of capitalism, would
be replaced by products neither bought nor sold but "simply
stored in communal warehouses and subsequently delivered
to those who need them." Socialism was defined as incomplete communism, during which, by degrees, "a moneyless
system of account-keeping will come to prevail."[8] In the
period of transition from capitalism to communism, "prices,
wages, profits, etc., at the same time exist and do not exist."[9]
Money, as a medium of exchange and as a unit of account, is
"expelled" from the socialist state sector, where resources
are allocated and goods are produced and interchanged according to a plan; in this sector there are neither market relations nor commodities.

Since the Marxists of this school affirmed that economics
could be concerned only with the study of the forces regu-
lating productive relationships in commodity-producing societies, economics and its principles were deemed to have
little to offer to the socialist planner. The tools of the latter
were to be material accounting and engineering rather than
economics. On the other hand, so long as market relations
subsisted in certain sectors, the "blind" forces typical of commodity-producing societies would continue to operate in
them. In these sectors the "law of value"—the "internal" law
subsuming the interaction of all the elemental forces which
regulate allocation of resources, production, and trade in
commodity-producing societies[10]—would hold sway. Socialism was envisaged as the combat ground of a new, conscious,
economic regulator, the "planning principle," and of the old

"blind force," the law of value, operating in the opposing state and commodity-producing sectors respectively.

A systematic presentation of the theoretical position of what may be called the second Marxist school was presented in the early 1920's by I. I. Stepanov-Skvortsov and A. A. Bogdanov. Relying notably on Engels' *Anti-Dühring,* Stepanov affirmed that economics did in fact concern itself with "historically changing material," but that it abstracted from it both "laws specific to each particular stage in the development of production and exchange" and a number of "general laws concerning production and exchange in general."[11] Economics thus defined cannot be confined to the study of capitalism or to the "economic regularities of a capitalist-commodity society."[12] Going a step further, A. A. Bogdanov pointed out that it was nonsense to claim that under socialism "commodities, prices, wages, etc., exist and do not exist." Value categories, however determined, existed under socialism and would exist under communism. Planning, added Bogdanov, must be based on the "knowledge of the value of the product," of accumulation (capital formation), and of consumption—otherwise no economic organization would be possible.[13] Bogdanov thus asserted that planning without economic accounting was impossible and that the planner had necessarily to take into consideration the "law of value," i.e., costs of production, uses of capital in alternative directions, objective limits of the pace of growth, and so on.

Rejecting Stepanov's arguments, Bukharin, Preobrazhenskii, Obolenskii-Ossinskii, and a number of other well-known Bolshevik leaders and economists—already sharply divided on specific matters of policy—stressed jointly that value (*tsennost'*) was "a category suitable only for a commodity-producing economy," and that in the Soviet Union "the vestiges of commodity-producing economy were in process of disappearance."[14] Answering Bogdanov, Preobrazhenskii, who was himself formulating some basic principles of Soviet policy, noted—in the mid 1920's!—that it may be feasible to formulate an economic theory of the period of transition but that such a theory will lose its significance under socialism, where "no political economy will be necessary."[15]

These theoretical contentions dominated Soviet thinking until 1929. By that time, as Stalin's fight against the Left Opposition (to which Preobrazhenskii belonged) and the Right Opposition (to which Bukharin belonged) reached its climax, the Bukharin-Preobrazhenskii positions in the economic field were also brought under serious scrutiny. Practice had in the meantime shown that the Soviet economy could hardly function in any other way than as a monetary economy. It became useful to the party to unearth Lenin's critical marginal notes on Bukharin's book, *Economics of the Transition Period,* to discard some of the earlier theories on economics in general and its application under socialism in particular, and to recognize the relevance of certain "general laws concerning production and exchange in general." But the party did not either admit at the time that socialism was a mere "commodity-producing" system such as capitalism had been, or indicate which "general laws" were applicable, and how, to the socialist system.[16] The formal recognition of the broad scope of economics—as suggested earlier by Stepanov—stressed the predominance within the state sphere of the "planning principle" (which for all practical purposes is the free will of the bureaucracy) and, in the sectors at the margin of the state complex, the predominance of the "law of value" (market relationships). The bureaucracy had thus agreed to broaden the sphere of "economics" but only so long as the latter did not interfere with its own ideas about ordering outputs, allocating resources, and dividing the national product.

By 1950, as the absurdities of bureaucratic improvisation —notably in the sphere of pricing—became more and more outrageous, Stalin himself had to challenge openly the smugness of the bureaucrats whom he had so long flattered. In his last writing, *Economic Problems of Socialism in the USSR*, Stalin repeated the nearly ritual phrase that under the Soviet system capital goods "can certainly not be classed in the category of commodities." But then, looking at Soviet reality, he added: "Why in that case do we speak of the value of means of production, their cost of production, their price, etc.?" This situation, Stalin continued, arises notably because *"consumers' goods,* which are needed to compensate . . . labor, are produced and realized in our country as commodities,"[17] and further, because the whole system requires "calculation and settlement, for determining whether enterprises are paying or running at a loss, for checking and controlling the enterprises."[18] While the "law of value" does not regulate production in the state sphere, value calculations do and must occur in that sphere. The trouble, concluded Stalin, "is not that the law operates in the socialist sphere" but that the Soviet managers do not "study it enough," a fact which explains the confusion reigning in Soviet price-fixing policy.[19] Thus, up to the early 1950's, notwithstanding the acceptance of a broader definition of economics, many of the theoretical contentions advanced in the early 1920's concerning the economic nature of socialism and its "laws" still remained unchallenged.[20]

By 1957, breaking away from Stalin's specious reasoning, the Polish economist Oskar Lange reasserted in full, but in a new form, the Skvortsov-Bogdanov positions. In a lecture, "On the Political Economy of Socialism," delivered in Belgrade,[21] Lange suggested that there were four types of economic "laws" operating under socialism: those which are general "in the sense that they operate in every socio-economic system;" those which are specific to the socialist mode of production; those which are of an intermediate nature, e.g., those which result from commodity production and monetary circulation; and finally, those which change as the administrative and managerial superstructure changes. Lange classified among his "general laws" the old "law of production and reproduction," which indicates that one cannot have his cake and eat it too, or, as Professor Lange put it, "that one cannot accumulate if one consumes the whole net product."[22] Further, added Lange, socialist production remains *commodity production,* given the multiplicity of owners of products in the socialist society and the distribution of its goods. The ownership of the means of production allows to the state two crucial things but those only: to determine the purposes for which the means of production are to be used, and to put economic activity to use for "satisfaction of the needs of society." But this ownership does not free the planner from cost-price considerations or from the "law of value," which asserts itself because socialism remains a commodity-producing system. Thus Professor Lange reintroduced under socialism not only all the value categories but also the general or "intermediate" laws of "political economy" of all commodity-producing, monetary societies.

The passage of the whole bourgeois economics camel through the eye of the socialist needle was apparently done successfully, since shortly after Professor Lange's lecture various Soviet economists "condemned" Stalin's economic errors and asserted that socialism was indeed an authentic "commodity-producing society." By the beginning of the 1960's one could finally read in a new official textbook, *Political Economy of Socialism,* edited by Professor K. N. Shafiev, that commodity-monetary relations are an "objective necessity" under socialism because various types of enterprises exist in this system. Shafiev and his collaborators stressed the obvious when they noted that recognition of the economic "autonomy" of each state enterprise requires the establishment of commodity-monetary relations among them, even though this autonomy differs from private ownership. The question of the disappearance of commodity relations was finally relegated to the distant and blessed future, when "the forces of production will reach the highest level of their development."[23] Shafiev adds that a number of economic laws may hold for various types of society. For instance, a so-called law of preferential increase of the output of capital goods is supposed to apply to a number of societies not otherwise specified. Finally, Shafiev adds that the basic laws of socialism and of communism are henceforth that "demand and wants increase jointly with the expansion of the possibility of fulfilling them, thus serving as inducement for further expansion of production."[24]

Until the appearance of Shafiev's text, official Soviet theory was based on the postulate that communism will be the reign of abundance, when production exceeds wants; but now it seems that both production and wants grow at the same time, with at least the possibility that the latter may exceed the former. This brings Soviet economics close to the idea of scarcity on which Western economics rests.

The discussions of Soviet policy makers and economists may appear as a sort of theological disputation remotely relevant to the matter in hand. Actually, the discussions had important practical and theoretical consequences. The idea of the early twenties that money was being "expelled" from the state sector, and that it would be ultimately expelled from the economy as a whole, had crucial consequences in respect to the structural organization of the economy and to planning procedure. In banking it led to a sharp distinction between inter-industry transactions—to be carried exclusively under the form of deposits—and all other transactions, to be carried out in currency. The circular flow was neatly bisected and placed under different types of controls.[25] In planning, it led to emphasis on physical programming of production and distribution, insuring the automatic carrying out of the over-all investment target as well as of the specific key output targets set by the policy makers.

The idea that the "law of value" was also being "expelled" from the state sector had mostly unfavorable results. It freed the planner from all inhibitions in scheduling great projects of expansion, but it encouraged fantastic price distortions, blunted the use of prices for allocative purposes, and bred waste in innumerable forms. The Soviet policy makers and planners thus developed a workable, and from numerous points of view ingenious, system of accounting and economic controlling, while at the same time they continued to remain

unaware of the deeper problem of rational allocation of resources.[26] The second main idea of the early twenties, that
planning and market relations are complete opposites and
that the former supersedes the latter—"crowds them out of
the economy"—precluded the utilization of central planning
in an imaginative way and rendered Soviet planning extremely inflexible for many years. The idea that economics,
and particularly "economics of capitalism," had little to offer
to the planner led to the elimination of the economist from
the preparation and organization of planning, and to his replacement by engineers and technicians who approached the
matter of optimal allocation of resources only from a narrow
technical point of view. This idea led to the rapid dessication
of Soviet economic thinking and to its complete divorce from
the main currents of Western economic thought.

Notwithstanding the differences between adherents of
"voluntarism" and "determinism," all Soviet Marxists shared
the belief that the basic activities of any society—including a
socialist one—are ultimately determined by that society's
mode of production. All were therefore convinced of the
need to expand the country's productive capacity, to increase
its industrial labor force, and to raise its over-all technological level. To some leaders these tasks appeared as particularly urgent, since they viewed with apprehension the prospects of the so-called "alliance" between the small number
of industrial workers and the vast mass of peasants, on which
the regime depended. In order to understand the prevailing
socio-economic relations in production and to map the path
of the economy's eventual expansion, a number of Soviet
economists turned their attention to Marx's famous macro-

economic model of "simple and enlarged reproduction," in which Marx presents (in the second volume of *Capital*[27]) the relation between sectors of production and between investment and growth in an abstractly defined capitalist economy. Taking Marx's schema as a point of departure, some Soviet economists constructed a number of interesting macro-economic models adapted to the Soviet economy of the time. These models attempted to clarify: the impact on growth of various patterns of distribution of investments between the capital goods and the consumers' goods industries (e.g., G. A. Fel'dman's model); the interrelations between sectors with different systems of ownership and production methods (E. A. Preobrazhenskii's model); the structural interdependence of the economy, i.e., its input-output relationships (P. I. Popov's and L. Litoshenko's model). The Soviet economists tackled and solved a number of problems which were to be dealt with later in the West on different analytical bases. The works of Fel'dman, Preobrazhenskii, and Popov-Litoshenko parallel some of the works of Western economists such as E. D. Domar or Wassily Leontief, though they fail to match the latter in sophistication and diverge from them in their underlying assumptions.

Let us look closely at the starting point of these Soviet economists and at the ways in which they modified the original Marxian model. The Marxist schemata provide a simple framework for analyzing relations between the demand and supply of physical goods and relations between product and income. The economy's output is viewed as being produced by two sectors, sector I producing capital goods and raw materials, and sector II producing consumers' goods. Gross value of output of each sector is equated to the sum of the gross sales of all its economic units, i.e., to each one's depreciation plus materials used, labor costs, and profits, or, alternatively, to each unit's expenditures on "means of production" (c), workers' wages (v), and "surplus value" achieved (m). The latter is spent by property owners either for their consumption only or both for consumption and for additional capital goods and manpower. Net product is obtained by eliminating c (depreciation and interfirm transactions) from gross sales, thus yielding a total similar to the net national product used in Western economic accounting, with the difference that it does not include services. In Marxian economics service income is visualized only as a set of transfers from the primary producers engaged in production of material or physical goods to secondary receivers. The net product, or net *material* product, is divided into "accumulation" (investment and increases in stocks and reserves) and consumption. Income generated in material production matches expenditures on producers' and consumers' goods—or accumulation plus consumption—since the outlays on services of primary income receivers are offset by the outlays on consumption of the secondary (service) income receivers. The schema yields finally a set of equations between the components of its aggregates (c, v, m, of I and II) under conditions either of zero net investment or of positive net investment.[28]

Thus Marx devised both an income accounting framework and a planning tool, effective, though in many respects crude, for ascertaining certain crucial macro-economic relationships and for scheduling certain economic balances in either repetitive or expanding economic conditions. In attempting to present in a simplified way the interrelations between income flows and balances between sectoral products,

Marx followed a tradition going back to the beginning of economics, namely, to the celebrated work of the physiocrat Francois Quesnay and his famous *Tableau économique*.

Starting from Marx's two-sector model, G. A. Fel'dman attempted to explore the necessary relations between investment, rate of growth of total capital, the capital coefficient (the ratio of output to capital), and rate of growth of each sector's product.[29] Fel'dman ingeniously modified Marx's model: he retained in a newly defined sector I (which he calls sector u) only the capacity-increasing activities of the economy, while he included in sector II (sector p) not only production of consumers' goods but also compensation for the wear and tear on the existing equipment, so that the output of that sector is maintained at its given level. By completely separating the two sectors, Fel'dman could posit that under repetitive conditions (i.e., in simple reproduction) sector u is inactive while total national product is produced by sector p. Under expanding conditions, sector u becomes active and provides equipment to cover the depreciation of its own capital stock and to increase the capital stock of either sector. Within this framework, the total capital (K) and the capital coefficient (S) of sector u determine rigidly the rate of investment, while the total capital and the capital coefficient of sector p determine the output of consumers' goods. In growth, the crucial variable in Fel'dman's model is the allocation of investment between the two sectors. If consumers' goods output is growing at a given rate, what conditions would be required for raising this rate to a higher level? Assuming invariant capital coefficients in both sectors, if all investment were to be directed to sector p, the output of sector u would be constant and the increments in total capital of sector p would remain constant. With constant increments in the capital stock of p, the *rate* of growth of the latter's output would be falling (always under the assumption of an unchanged ratio of output to capital). To keep the output p growing at a constant rate, a certain fraction of investments would have to be directed toward sector u and a certain relationship would have to be achieved between the increments in the total capital ($\triangle K$) of the two sectors. The rate of growth of sector u should neither fall below nor exceed the requirements of p. Fel'dman thus demonstrates that for this purpose, the marginal rate of growth of the total capital of u would necessarily have to equal the marginal rate of growth of the capital stock of p ($\triangle K_u = \triangle K_p$).

On the other hand, to raise the rate of growth of p's output, $\triangle K_u$ would have to *exceed* temporarily $\triangle K_p$. The latter should catch up with the former after the expanded capital stock of u could provide adequate increments for expanding K_p. The rate of growth of p's output could be expressed as a function of the ratio of the total capital of the two sectors, $\dfrac{K_u}{K_p}$, a ratio which Fel'dman calls the "structural index" of the economy and the expression of the "intensity of its industrialization." Beyond a certain value of $\dfrac{K_u}{K_p}$, the rate of growth of p's output may, however, hardly be increased. Always under the assumption of an invariant capital coefficient in u, the constant rate of growth of consumers' goods could not exceed the limit which this capital coefficient sets to it and which it approaches as the ratio $\dfrac{K_u}{K_p}$ approaches infinity.

Fel'dman then explores the relations between rates of growth of consumers' goods output, changes in the structural index of the economy, the capital coefficients, and the level of investment. After recalling that, by hypothesis, K_u and K_p cover both fixed assets and circulating capital, and that the raising of the capital coefficient S usually requires also an increase in working capital, Fel'dman removes the assumption of invariant coefficients and points out that: (1) with capital coefficients rising in both sectors apace, but in such a way that the structural index of the economy remains the same (that is, the "degree" of industrialization of the country is not changed), the rate of growth of p's output is given by the ratio $\dfrac{\triangle S_p}{S_p}$; (2) with the capital coefficient rising faster in u and in p, but in such a way that the economy's industrial index is also changed (i.e., that $\dfrac{K_u}{K_p}$ also increases), industrialization is accelerated and p's output grows more rapidly because of the given increase in p's capital coefficient and of the establishment of a more adequate relation between K_p and K_u—the rational development of the economy in the interest of consumption requiring a definite relationship between K_p and K_u for any given rate of growth of p; (3) with the capital coefficient rising faster in p than in u, but with the ratio $\dfrac{K_u}{K_p}$ declining, the rate of growth of p's output is depressed; Fel'dman shows then what investment rates would be required in order to achieve various growth rates in p's output, given various values of the ratio $\dfrac{K_u}{K_p}$ and various capital coefficients in both sectors.

Fel'dman thus attempted to show how with good mathematical logic the planners could, with the help of his two-sector model, formulate plan variants, and select the optimal one, once the policy makers had picked out a rate of growth for consumption (i.e., for p's output) and the technicians and statisticians had prepared adequate data concerning total capital and capital coefficients. One may of course question the realism of his model, though its basic device, the complete separation between the "capacity-increasing" sector and the rest of the economy, is actually not much more arbitrary than the more conventional division of output into investment and consumption. But Fel'dman's true merit consists in his novel exploration of the relations between allocation of investment, growth of capital stock, and growth of output—an exploration in which he anticipated some aspects of modern income growth analysis, for example, Professors Harrod and Domar's "warranted" or equilibrium rate of growth,[30]—and in his courage in pointing out, at the beginning of the Soviet industrialization euphoria, the existence of objective limits to growth rates no matter how huge the allocation of investment toward the capacity-increasing sector might be.

In the climate of the late 1920's Fel'dman's methodology, with its building blocks in value terms and its emphasis on final demand and capital coefficients, could find no grace in the eyes of the Soviet bureaucracy. The latter could not accept any objective standards for capital allocation. Fel'dman's model, as used for planning purposes by N. A. Kovalevskii, was therefore severely criticized, and Fel'dman's work was never again referred to in the Soviet economic literature; his model remained buried in the pages of *Planovoe khoziaistvo* until the late 1950's, when Professor Evsey

Domar dedicated to it a comprehensive and illuminating economic essay.[31]

Another interesting attempt to adapt Marx's schema for examination of some problems posed by the Soviet accelerated industrialization effort was carried out by Evgenii Preobrazhenskii in the mid-1920's. Preobrazhenskii set out to investigate the conditions of equilibrium which arise when the backward Soviet economy is geared by its policy makers and planners toward bridging both the wide technological gaps existing among its branches and the enormous gulf which separates it from the most advanced countries of the West.[32]

Preobrazhenskii expanded Marx's two-sector model into a six-sector model by splitting three ways Marx's producers' and consumers' goods sectors. Stressing that Marx had investigated the problems of growth within the framework of a pure capitalist economy and that in the backward Soviet economy sectoral interconnections were much more complex, Preobrazhenskii indicated that his three-way division corresponded to the existence within the Soviet economy of three distinct production systems: state, capitalist, and small-scale producers, definable as a function of their technology, outputs, and form of ownership. He identified sector I of the state complex with the whole of heavy industry; sector II of the state economy with certain branches of the light and food processing industries of national significance, e.g., the textile, leather, sugar, and alcohol industries; sectors I and II of capitalist production with the privately run producers' and consumers' goods industries of municipal significance; sector I of the small-scale producers' system with cottage industry and handicraft workshops; and sector II of this last system with, primarily, peasant agriculture. He then mapped the product flows between his three "production systems" and their six sectors. In the course of his demonstrations Preobrazhenskii treated the capitalist and small-scale producers as the unified private economy counterposed to the state complex, and thus reduced his own model to four sectors.

Defining the relations between the Marxian product and income categories (c, v, m) of each sector, Preobrazhenskii points out that in equilibrium: (a) the value of the capital goods purchased by sector II of the economy as a whole must equal the wage bill and the "nonproductive" consumption of state sector I; and (b) the value of the state-manufactured consumers' goods purchased by the wage earners and the "nonproductive" consumers of the private sector must equal the value of the expenditure of the wage earners of the state sectors on peasant produce. Otherwise, he notes, in the first case a shortage of producers' goods would appear, which would force an increase in imports, and in the second case a shortage of state-manufactured consumers' goods would arise—a so-called goods famine—which could be redressed only through taxation or through imports. Passing from a given level of capital formation in the state complex to a new higher level posits, according to Preobrazhenskii, a decline in capital formation in the private economy, and the incapacity of the latter adequately to supply raw materials to state sector II. Finally, the passage to a high capital formation in the crucial state sector I requires that a tribute be extracted from the private economy as a whole and particularly from the small-scale producers' sector II. Preobrazhenskii does not, however, define rigorously either the size of this tribute or its connection with changes in the rate of growth in the capital formation of state sector I.

Preobrazhenskii's model suggests various lines of attack in the study of growth in newly developing economies. The coexistence of sharply contrasting production and distribution complexes within the same economy—e.g., large state and private complexes with regional differences, modern and indigenous complexes—with different factor proportions, different investment capabilities, and differential growth rates raises a number of significant problems in the study of development. Preobrazhenskii's effort parallels some of the modern Western discussions on "technological dualism," though the respective points of departure and goals of demonstration are far apart. Preobrazhenskii is interested in the conditions for, and consequences of, accelerated growth of the (state) capital-intensive sector, and in the ways in which the divergencies between this sector and the rest of the economy may be used in designing development strategy. Western authors of sectored models aim usually at clarifying some typical phenomena of underdevelopment, such as the logic of further capital intensification in the modern sector, the redundancy of resources and hence the existence of unemployment at equilibrium, the inflationary consequences of attempts to develop, etc.[33] Preobrazhenskii's demonstrations unfortunately lack the depth of Fel'dman's essays, and hence fail to match the tight reasoning of modern growth models.[34]

A third interesting attempt to visualize the macro-economic relationships in the Soviet economy of the 1920's was made by P. I. Popov and L. N. Litoshenko. Popov and Litoshenko developed both from Marx's two-sector model and from the Soviet practice of drawing "balances" of resources and allocation for specific products the idea of a detailed intersectoral input-output matrix of the economy as a whole. In explaining their method in a crucial study, "The balance of the national economy of the USSR for 1923/24,"[35] the authors noted that (a) any economy, whatever its social form, necessarily is based on an equilibrium system resulting from mutually interacting supply and demand relationships in production and distribution in each branch, among branches, and among "social classes;" and that (b) the task of the statistician is to show precisely how and in what forms this equilibrium was achieved or disturbed, and how economic relationships among enterprises and "classes" was concretely established. For this specific purpose Marx's abstract model—with its bisector division of output according to its destination to producers or consumers and its over-all balancing of the supply and demand of all producers' and consumers' goods respectively—was far from appropriate. Equally inadequate was the usual type of social accounting tabulation dealing with value added in production. What was needed was first, to divide the economy into branches—or industries—by *product* (or group of products) of homogeneous significance for production or consumption; and second, to trace each of these products throughout the spheres of production as well as of distribution. What was thus envisaged was a way of tabulating simultaneously both inter-industry flows and final distribution of the net product.

In defining their approach to a new balance Popov, Litoshenko, and their collaborators stressed the identity of their concepts with those of Quesnay and Marx. But they added that the Marxian two-sector model was too abstract and too limiting to portray a system of general equilibrium in all its concrete aspects at a given historical moment. They decided, therefore, to subdivide the economy into a large number of branches defined according to their type of product rather than according to whether their products were utilized by other industries or by ultimate consumers. They stressed that they viewed all activities of the national economy as a whole, as a unique process fusing all purchases and sales of each and every sector of "material production." A basic flow matrix identified within agriculture and industry the following types of outputs (and imports): (a) consumer goods, (b) raw and other materials, (c) fuels, and (d) tools of production. It detailed their distribution in the spheres of "productive consumption" (interbranch transactions in agriculture, industry, construction, transportation, and trade), and of "nonproductive consumption" (individual consumption and government), and finally indicated the amount exported. Supporting tables identified a number of branches in each sector (eight in agriculture, three in mining, and eleven in industry), as well as a number of products, and detailed interbranch purchases and sales. The basic balance presented simultaneously, as Litoshenko put it, the "turnover record" of the economy as a whole and the "credit-debit" operation of each industry.

Popov and his collaborators thus grasped the advantages of a statistical framework that would lace together the entire economic system, and then adroitly tabulated for the purpose gross rather than net outputs. They recorded all users of output—the producing branch itself, other producing branches, and final consumers—and succeeded in revealing for the first time the concurrent input-output aspects of the operations of each branch and sector as they merged with the processes of production and consumption of the economy as a whole. They forged a new statistical tool, still crude but with large potentialities, as appeared subsequently when Professor Wassily Leontief used a similar type of analysis and generalized it in an appropriate algebraic form. Popov and Litoshenko failed to reach the level of sophistication and versatility which present-day input-output analysis has achieved through the use of matrix algebra; but this does not mean that they should be denied their rightful title of pioneers.

In the light of the pioneering character of their methodology it may be interesting to recall the reactions which the Balance provoked, both in Soviet official circles and abroad. Neither the Balance's methodology nor its conclusions were considered of much use for Soviet planning. In 1925 S. G. Strumilin, the spokesman of Soviet officialdom, boasted that the Central Statistical Administration was compiling its Balance "through the initiative of the State Planning Committee, which had provided the outline and the main methodological instructions for its compilation,"[36] but by the time the Balance came out Strumilin disclaimed any connection with the results. The whole work was dismissed as simply "a game with figures" and the discussion on how to draw an appropriate balance was continued for a while with much intensity, since, as the *Vestnik statistiki* put it in 1927, "such a balance does not yet exist."[37]

In presenting his own suggestion for a balance, one of the most celebrated economists of the early twenties, V. G. Groman, criticized Popov for failing to encompass in a single table stocks as well as flows, outlays of manpower and of mechanical energy, and class divisions. After dismissing

Popov's work as having "little in common with Quesnay or Marx," Groman added: "the most essential idea of a balance —the organic unity of all fundamental factors: production, distribution, exchange, and consumption—remains therefore unrealized." Groman's own proposals clearly reveal his lack of understanding of the novel implications of the Popov-Litoshenko approach.[38]

Strangely enough, Professor Wassily Leontief himself— then a young student abroad—also reviewed in a brief paper, published in 1925, the basic ideas of the Balance as presented by Popov, in a preliminary but fairly detailed report on his work.[39] While stressing that the Balance represented an important work, Leontief attacked Popov and Litoshenko's procedures mainly on the following counts: for restricting the scope of the inquiry to material accounting (excluding services) and for using "total turnover" data (gross output figures), which, said Leontief, multiply double counting. He specifically rejected as "wholly wrong" the method of the "technical dissecting" of agriculture into branches, since, as he put it, this further multiplied the double counting. In conclusion, Leontief recommended the construction of net product tabulations instead, thus missing in his first contact with the Balance method the gist of its novelty and future importance.

While the policy makers were quarreling on the questions of how to change the Soviet society's socio-economic parameters, what direction of development to impart to the state sector and to its industry, and how to increase the over-all level of capital formation, the economists could not reach any agreement on the nature of the working principles of

the Soviet economy and its *modus operandi*. Both pragma-
tists and doctrinaires—the former interested in safeguarding
the regime's freedom of "economic maneuver," the latter
bogged down in Marx's labor theory of value—violently attacked Popov's, Preobrazhenskii's, and Fel'dman's models.
The concept of general equilibrium between supply and demand in each and every branch, and between production
and distribution as a whole, became anathema to Stalin's
leadership and to its central planners; the idea that objective restraints ("economic laws") operating under capitalism
could assert themselves under the Soviet regime and could
limit its "maneuverability" was denounced as "bourgeois
economics." Popov, branded as "impractical," was deposed
as director of the Central Statistical Administration. Litoshenko, a pioneer in social accounting, was attacked viciously
for having dared to state that one could not say anything
about the (socialist or capitalist) "mechanism which creates
a mass of products" by simply looking at the national income
accounts.[40] Preobrazhenskii, under fire for a number of reasons with which we shall deal later on, was also denounced
for embracing the idea of "equilibrium" and for spelling out
how equilibrium could be maintained if the economy were
to grow rapidly. Finally, Fel'dman, along with those who
attempted to use his ideas for planning purposes—N. A. Kovalevskii, for instance—, came under attack for stressing that
"laws of production are independent of *any* social system."
The idea that in *any* society the rate of investment and pattern of its distribution affect the growth of national income
was branded as "Bogdanovism"—"bourgeois economics."[41]

The hostility of the leaders in power toward economic analysis and model building, toward the application of mathe-

matical methods, toward the idea of the universality of economic principles hampered for decades the development of economic thought, particularly under the long rule of Stalin. While input-output analysis grew vigorously in the West, it was discarded in its infancy in the USSR, where one might have expected it to be developed and used for planning purposes. An interesting effort of M. Barengol'ts to find out the ratios of inputs to output—the technical coefficients of production—in order to determine what he called the "dynamics of interindustry consumption of the products of agriculture and forestry" put an end, for a few decades, to Soviet attempts to further input-output analysis.[42] It is therefore utterly ridiculous to claim now—as does the Soviet statistician Riabushkin, for instance—that "bourgeois statistics" are now "considerably behind Soviet statistics in solving the problems of balance sheets for the simple reason of the superiority of organization and methods used in the USSR."[43] It is also gratuitous to claim that Soviet planning and accounting would have brought the pioneering schemes of Popov, Litoshenko, and Barengol'ts to maturity, that is, to the level of Western input-output analysis; the pretense than an "uninterrupted" line exists between this early work and the current Soviet uses of input-output analysis[44] is of course completely unacceptable. Even though, initially, the idea of input-output was sparked by Soviet statisticians some four decades ago, progress in this direction was prevented in the USSR. In fact, the Russians can now borrow a fully developed method, precisely because Western economists did not need to pay any attention to Soviet economic edicts.

3 Strategies of Economic Development

STRATEGIES are ways of using resources in order to secure
a given long-run objective, political, economic, or military.
In war, as von Clausewitz explains, strategy is the general
plan which links together the series of acts that are to lead
to the final military decision. In time of peace the leaders
of a market-directed economy do not need to have a fully
integrated set of national economic goals, or to forge an integrated, all-embracing economic strategy. These leaders
may have a number of economic policies, often conflicting
ones, and a number of flexible strategies for meeting them.[1]
In war, all policies and strategies are dominated by the overriding goal of victory. Then the market mechanism is seriously tampered with in order to ensure that the bulk of the
country's resources will be rapidly channeled to fulfill the
needs of waging and winning the war. On the other hand, in
the normal conditions of their operations, every enterprise
must have some short-run, intermediate, or long-run objective concerning output and growth, and a broad strategy for
reaching these goals. Usually the big corporations have well-
planned long-run objectives concerning output, expansion,
and diversification based on forecasts and expectations con-

cerning prices and the activity of competing firms or of related branches.

The Soviet economy may be likened to a single multi-branch, multi-plant corporation with a fixed, overriding goal, that of catching up with and surpassing the highest productive indices of capitalism, i.e., the indices reached by the economy of the United States. This goal was officially proclaimed in 1925 as the basic goal of Soviet economic policy. We should recall here that according to Marx's theories, socialism should by definition be more productive than the system which it displaces. Some persons, like the so-called Left Opposition of the Russian Communist Party headed by Leon Trotsky, stressed this tenet repeatedly from the early 1920's on, and affirmed that socialism could actually triumph only on a world scale and certainly could never be "completed" in a backward economy lagging far behind capitalism in productivity. The Left therefore affirmed the need to establish within this backward economy the "dictatorship of industry" as the unique lever of internal socio-economic change, and propounded world revolution as the only lever for changing the relationships of forces between the USSR and the rest of the world. Other members of the Communist party, most of whom were to be later connected with the so-called Right Opposition identified with Nikolai Bukharin, posited that full socialism could be constructed within the frontiers of a single country, even at "a turtle's pace," whatever the backwardness of the economic structure inherited from capitalism. But some of the Communists of the Right —G. Y. Sokolnikov, for instance—maintained that the USSR could not build socialism in isolation, since no country could sever itself from the rest of the world, hide behind a monopoly of foreign trade, and keep on trailing in productivity behind the rest of the world.

Those who, like Stalin, were soon to be identified with a "Center" tendency in the party's leadership, and who placed their entire faith in the political might gained by the party's machine in Russia, embarrassed themselves little with bookish definitions of socialism. They took over the tenets of Bukharin and soon affirmed not only that socialism was in construction in the USSR but that this construction was rapidly being finished. By 1937 they officially proclaimed in effect that socialism had been "completed," though the country continued to lag in output and in productivity on almost all counts in comparison with capitalism.

The deep cleavage between those who stressed the impossibility of building socialism in an isolated and backward country and those who proclaimed the possibility of building socialism in isolation had enormous consequences in the political field. Paradoxically, in the economic field these divergences did not prevent all factions in the mid-1920's from subscribing to the same overriding goal of industrialization. All affirmed their desire to expand substantially the country's productive capacity and to shift Soviet industry and with it the Soviet economy as a whole onto a "higher technological plane." The Left did so primarily because of its belief in the absolute necessity of establishing the "dictatorship of industry" in order to maintain the "dictatorship of the proletariat;" the Right did so because of its conviction that an appropriate type of industrialization would provide the best cement for the "workers' and peasants' alliance" and would stabilize the regime; the so-called Center did so because it saw in industrialization a lever for consolidating its own political power inside the USSR, and for guaranteeing Russia's military position *vis-à-vis* the neighboring capitalist powers.

But broad agreement on a long-run, overriding goal of industrialization did not imply agreement on the immediate *pace* of capital formation in the economy as a whole, and in each sector in particular; on the *methods* of mobilizing resources for the purpose, e.g., voluntary or forced saving; or, finally, on the specific development pattern to be followed by setting up priorities for this or that sector or for this or that industrial branch. The question of the choice of pace, methods, and pattern of development depended on the specific weight assigned by the policy makers to a number of political, social, and economic "proximate" (or intermediate) ends, such as the importance of industrial workers in the total labor force, the relationships between state-owned industry and privately owned agriculture, etc. The set of decisions on pace, pattern, and methods of development, taken on the basis of various assumptions concerning the relationship among intermediate ends and the ultimate goal of industrialization, forms what may be called the Soviet *strategy* of economic development.

The relationships between agriculture and industry and their respective rates of savings, capital formation, productivity, capital output ratios, and so on, are of crucial importance for all countries starting on the path of economic development. The relationships lose, however, in significance when the weight of agriculture as a sector decreases within developed, industrialized economies. Writing at the end of the eighteenth century or during the first half of the nineteenth, the classical economists naturally paid close attention to sectoral growth and to differences between industry and agriculture. They placed the distinction between these two sectors at the heart of their analysis of growth. Assuming that agriculture operated under the law of diminishing returns, while industry on the other hand operated under the sign of constant or increasing returns to scale, they viewed agriculture as the sector placing the ultimate limits on both economic growth and population growth. For obvious reasons, theories and models of growth for advanced countries have since taken new paths and have discarded as insufficiently enlightening the interactions of industry and agriculture.

Following the classical tradition, Marx also drew a sharp contrast between the significance of industry and that of agriculture in the process of growth. But he viewed their interrelationships dynamically: he assumed that agriculture would ultimately be fully industrialized, so that it would be, so to speak, sucked in by industry. In his growth model—his so-called schema of simple and enlarged reproduction, which we have already discussed—Marx no longer distinguishes between industry and agriculture; instead he separates the total production of the society into two "departments" (or sectors): the sector of means of production and the sector of articles of consumption. All the various branches of production belong to one of these two sectors in the Marxian model, which applies to an abstract, fully developed "commodity society."

Using the Marxian approach for analyzing the development of capitalism in Russia at the end of the nineteenth century, Lenin asserted in a detailed attack against the theories of the Russian Populists (Narodniki) that economic growth posited what we may call economic transformation as well as certain "necessary" relations between the producers' and the consumers' goods sectors.[2] For Lenin, transformation meant both the continuous growth of the industrial population at the expense of the agricultural one, and the ultimate industrialization of agriculture itself. Smooth development, on the other hand, required specific relationships between Marx's two sectors and their components. Working out the relationships of the Marxian model, Lenin affirmed that: (a) the limits of growth are necessarily set for a closed economy by the excess of its producers' goods output over its consumption of capital and raw materials; (b) that in the process of development the typical elements are the multiplication of interindustry transactions and the expansion of the demand for producers' goods, rather than the demand for consumers' goods;[3] (c) in growth, the "organic composition" of capital "necessarily" changes in such a way that the increment of expenditures on capital goods over the increment of expenditures on labor increases in both sectors, and at a faster rate in the first than in the second sector.[4] Though some of Lenin's propositions are questionable,[5] they were viewed by Bolsheviks of all factions as uncovering the mainsprings of growth. It was not easy to determine, however, to what extent the relationships occurring in a capitalist "commodity economy" applied in the USSR of the mid-1920's. The Bolsheviks were evidently ready and willing to increase capital accumulation rapidly and to make vast changes in the systems of ownership and production. But in trying to reshuffle the socio-economic parameters they had to take into account first the relationship between the state-managed in-

dustrial complex—particularly its large-scale industrial com-
ponent—and privately owned small-scale agriculture, and
second, the political relations between the Soviet state machine as a whole and the vast mass of the peasantry. The
prevailing and prospective relationship between (state) industry and (private) agriculture became a controversial
question as the policy makers prepared to gear the economy
for rapid growth.

The problems of the interrelations between industry and
agriculture in respect to savings, investment, and growth
were extensively examined during two crucial debates. The
first, on the so-called "scissors" crisis, opened in the summer
of 1923 and closed formally in 1924; the second, on mobilization of investible resources, on pace and pattern of capital
formation, opened in 1925 and closed formally by the end
of 1928. Both debates are of great interest not only for understanding the evolution of the USSR but also for grasping
some of the problems which in the underdeveloped countries
today face the policy makers and planners who set their
sights on rapid economic growth.

The so-called "scissors" crisis of the summer of 1923, which
marked, as Maurice Dobb puts it, "the parting of the ways
between two fundamentally different views," concerned
both the policy introduced since the beginning of 1921 under the famous name of New Economic Policy (NEP) and
the general orientation of the regime in respect to economic
development during the whole period of transition between
capitalism and socialism.[6] The crisis took its name from
a very sharp reversal in the "terms of trade" between industry and agriculture, or between town and village, from 1922
to 1923; graphically, the price trends suggested an opened

scissors. In 1922 the exchange ratio of agricultural to manufactured goods had favored the peasantry and had induced it to increase the sown area and grain output; but in the summer of 1923 the index of industrial prices rose sharply while that of agriculture fell substantially. A widening gap developed between industrial and agricultural prices, which threatened the modest progress that had been achieved, stirred up the peasantry, and imperiled the supplies of raw materials to industry and of grain to the towns.

A number of first-rank leaders of the party, and a number of economists and officials who sided with them, attributed the crisis to the "increasing disproportion" between the very slowly recovering industry and the rapidly expanding agriculture. Industry was operating below capacity levels, with obsolete equipment, and within an "anarchic" (free) market with no central coordination. This faction, which presented its views under Trotsky's banner of "dictatorship of industry,"[7] advocated the maintenance of high industrial prices and of large state subsidies in order to accelerate the retooling of industry and the increase of its output; it also proposed centralized planning in order to achieve a better intersector coordination. Those who criticized this so-called "industrialist" tendency, and who represented at the time the majority of the party and of public opinion, affirmed that the crisis had arisen because of state industry's abuse of its monopolistic power, an abuse practiced without any regard to either the political or the economic long-run consequences of such a policy. This interpretation affirmed that industry was deliberately forcing the terms of trade in its favor and for the purpose was producing a small output of consumers' goods, that is, it was generating a "goods famine." The "anti-industrialists" requested that the crisis be solved by curbing industry's managers, decreasing prices, and orienting industrial output not toward heavy goods but toward the specific type of goods needed by the peasant market.

The debate on the scissors crisis and the following debate on industrialization were deeply intertwined with other political discussions among the Communist leaders on a number of decisive internal and international problems which fall outside the scope of this essay. The economic positions of the Left—presented in elaborate form by Piatakov and Preobrazhenskii—were rejected by the leadership of the party early in 1924. The Thirteenth Party Conference in January 1924 condemned the over-all policy of the industrial managers, their price rises and the abuse of their monopoly power in the market, stressed the dependence of industry's growth on the situation of peasant agriculture, and affirmed that this dependence could be changed "only by political and economic changes in the industrial countries of Europe" —not within the USSR alone.[8] The party leadership decided to close the "scissors'" blades by lowering industrial prices and by letting agricultural prices rise.

The so-called industrialization debate grew out of the scissors crisis, and raised in an even more acute form the same problems. This time the debate was prompted by (1) the continuing and prospective aggravation of the shortage of manufactured goods of large consumption—the so-called "goods famine;" (2) the pressing need for renewing capital equipment in industry, the latter having used up by the end of 1925—as the then President of the Supreme Economic Council, Felix Dzerzinski, put it—"all the capital bequeathed to us by the bourgeoisie, whether in funds, buildings, or materials;" (3) the necessity of mapping at the close of the period of postwar recovery some specific ways toward the "reconstruction" of the economy, that is, toward the introduction of new processes, new equipment, and even new industrial branches.[9] The debate put again, in a more virulent form, the question at what pace industry and agriculture should develop, in what ways investible resources should be mobilized, and finally, what specific pattern of allocation of resources between industrial branches should be chosen.

Two basic strategies emerged among the solutions proposed. The first—which may be designated as the Right-wing strategy—stressed the importance of peasant output and peasant demand for consumers' goods. It advocated the priority development of agriculture and of the special branches of industry which cater to peasant demand. The Left-wing strategy emphasized the importance of industry and of the latter's own demand for capital goods. It advocated the rapid development of industry in general and of the heavy industrial branches in particular, and to this end suggested that real savings should be transferred from agriculture to industry. This Left-wing strategy, which was adopted after a set of maneuvers that led to the crushing of both Left and Right by the party's "Center" under Stalin, was proclaimed to be the "Soviet method of industrialization." Let us consider the main arguments advanced during this debate, since the discussion clarifies the underlying assumptions and the basic tenets of the strategy of development applied unflinchingly by the Soviet leadership since then.

The Right was strongly influenced by the writings of various professional economists and experts who stressed the

importance of a flourishing agriculture in order to expand
the domestic market and to establish a broad-based connection with the world market. Outstanding among these economists was Lev Shanin, who presented in its most elaborate
form the case against "forced" industrialization.[10] Address-
ing himself to the immediate problem of the "goods famine,"
Shanin affirmed that the crisis was generated by the discrep-
ancy between the patterns of investment and of demand. The
state industry, said Shanin, is emphasizing output of capital
goods in the face of an expanding peasant demand for consumers' goods, a demand sustained by increased peasant
sales of raw materials and grain. Shanin suggested that heavy
industry was, in the given conditions, developing too fast,
and that industrial investment ought to be reoriented toward
the light industrial branches in order to meet the peasant demand. To avoid goods shortages, investment in heavy industry should be postponed until large inventories of manufactured consumers' goods could be built up either through the
activity of domestic industries or through importation. In the
meantime the bulk of investible resources should be oriented
toward agriculture, since the latter could absorb more labor
per unit of capital invested, could yield more per unit invested because it had low capital-output ratios, and could
build up large savings on account of its low consumption
rates. Part of these savings, added Shanin, could be subsequently tapped for investment in industry. Assuming a profit
of 6 per cent in industry as compared to 15 per cent in agriculture, Shanin asserted that a hundred units of capital "di-
verted" from agriculture to industry in one year would
amount the following year to 106 additional units in industry,
the third year to 112.3, the fourth year to 119.1; whereas if
the original 100 units were left in agriculture they would

total 115 units the following year, 132.2 the third year, and 152.0 the fourth year.

Shanin concluded that by reinvesting in agriculture and by postponing the diversion of its resources toward industry, the latter could subsequently develop at a more rapid pace. The growth of agriculture would finally allow the expansion of the economy as a whole. Since foreign trade would be intensified and stocks of consumers' goods would be accumulated, industry could finally forge ahead in new directions without causing commodity shortages. For Shanin, the best sequence to be followed to keep the country on the path of growth was the traditional one: starting with the development of agriculture, continuing with the development of agricultural industries working for export, then with the growth of light industries supplying the domestic market, and ending up, at the appropriate moment, with the expansion of heavy industries when an additional demand for consumers' goods created by the increased employment in the producers' goods branches could be fully satisfied. Shanin's thesis thus implied continuous concern with the adequacy of *aggregate* demand for the Soviet economy's product, a preoccupation which had loomed large during the so-called scissors crisis. Actually, as Soviet industrialization got under way, this problem receded into the background and finally lost all significance. Insufficiency of aggregate demand is not a serious problem in an industrializing underdeveloped area.

While accepting some of Shanin's assumptions, Bukharin —first the party's whip against the Left wing, later the spokesman of the Right Opposition—rejected outright Shanin's "indefinite" postponement of investments in certain industrial branches. Bukharin affirmed that the state necessarily had to tap part of the savings accumulated in agriculture for the sake of the development of industry. What he considered crucial, however, was the "optimal" size of such a transfer; the aim for him was securing optimal growth of both sectors. Rephrasing Shanin, Bukharin wrote: "the most rapid pace of growth of industrial development does not depend at all on the maximum funds which we take out of agriculture. This matter is not that simple. If we take less today, we allow a larger accumulation in agriculture and at the same time we insure a larger demand for the products of our industry tomorrow. Thanks to the increased income in agriculture, we shall be able to take from it more next year than in the past, and we shall insure a higher growth in future years and even higher achievements for our state industry."[11]

The cornerstone of Bukharin's argument is that industry depends on both agricultural supply and peasant demand, but that agriculture in turn needs not only manufactured goods of mass consumption but agricultural machinery as well. The limits of industry's growth are directly governed by the growth of agricultural output in grain, cotton, hides, wool, flax, and so on. Reduction in grain output means a shrinkage of exports and consequently of imports of the capital goods with which to start the "reconstruction;" while reduction in output of agricultural materials reduces the output of domestically manufactured consumers' goods. Bukharin rejected the affirmation of the industrialists, according to whom "industry was lagging behind agriculture," and he added that industry could easily lower its prices by reducing waste, inefficiency, and bureaucratism, and by checking the danger of abusing monopoly power. "Industry," added Bukharin, "will develop faster if we accelerate the circulation of commodities between town and countryside. If this trade becomes more active, the total of our profits will grow at the same price or even with lower prices."[12] During the initial period of reconstruction, agriculture will provide the means with which equipment can be imported from abroad. But a domestic heavy industry will have to be developed in order to render the country independent of the world market and to transform agriculture into a more productive sector. Bukharin's advocacy of the need to develop heavy industry along with light industry became the party line at the Fifteenth All-Union Party Conference in November 1926.[13]

The party's Left wing led an all-out attack against Shanin's theses and against Bukharin's theories. The Left's economic arguments were developed by E. A. Preobrazhenskii, shortly after the scissors crisis, in a number of articles published in 1924 and 1925 and reprinted in 1926 in his book *Novaia ekonomika* (*New Economics*).[14] *New Economics* remains a basic document for an understanding of the foundations of the Soviet theory of economic growth. Discarding Shanin's arguments on the advantages of higher returns immediately obtainable from investing in agriculture, Preobrazhenskii affirmed that the introduction of production techniques equal or superior to those of capitalism would be possible only by securing a high rate of capital accumulation and, in the conditions of the USSR, by achieving a high degree of concentration of investments in the producers' goods industries. Ultimately, he added, reductions in the prices of goods of mass consumption will be secured by reducing the prices of capital goods needed by the consumers' goods industries. Positing that the establishment of a "new technical base as . . . underpinning for the complex of the state economy" requires the introduction of capital-intensive methods of production—though capital may be scarce relative to labor[15]—, Preobrazhenskii held that large-scale production is actually less wasteful than small-scale production, since the latter ties up larger amounts of resources in its production cycle for longer periods.[16] While the technical basis of industry is being revamped, maximum protection must be provided against the pressures of the "still stronger" capitalist economy.

Until Soviet industry bridged the gap between its productivity and that of the most advanced countries, agriculture must remain highly labor-intensive: this, states Preobrazhenskii, is the inevitable "penalty of underdevelopment."[17] But once the heavy industry branches are fully modernized, a vast transformation of agriculture and of the economy as a whole along new lines becomes possible.[18] During the decades in which the productivity of Soviet industry lags behind that of the most developed capitalist country, the United States, the massive investments required for retooling and modernization will have to be extracted from agriculture by a variety of means. Preobrazhenskii defined this long period as the "infant stage of development of the socialist industry," and asserted that the more backward a socialist country, the greater is the importance of small-scale ownership in its economy, and the more heavily its "socialist accumulation" will have to depend on a massive diversion of savings (surplus production) from agriculture to industry. This, said Preobrazhenskii, is "the law of primitive socialist accumulation," holding sway throughout the "infant stage of development of the socialist industry." Preobrazhenskii posited (a) that potential savings exceed actual savings in agriculture, (b) that the investment needed for retooling the state industry, moving it onto the "highest technological plane," and expanding it is for all practical purposes unlimited (that is, employment opportunities in industry are determined by the availability of capital rather than by the demand for output), and finally (c) that peasant demand is therefore of secondary importance and cannot provide the stimulus needed for large-scale industrial growth.

Following the premises of Preobrazhenskii, Piatakov and other leaders of the Left stressed repeatedly in the mid-twenties the idea that for the Soviet economy as a whole the question of stepped-up capital formation in industry was one of crucial importance, that industry had largely used up its previous capital, and that massive retooling was indispensable. Rejecting the idea that industry could continue to maintain the growth rates attained by it during the recovery period, Piatakov added that industry and agriculture had been in a wrong relationship before the war, and that there was no reason whatever for the Soviet regime to perpetuate this type of structural imbalance.[19] The Left therefore underlined the need for a swift reallocation of scarce resources in favor of industry and for a stepped-up rate of investment, taking for granted the ability of the regime to solve such thorny questions as how to secure the needed commodities, skills, and organization.[20]

The Left-wing position, dubbed in the early 1920's "super-industrialist," was at first resolutely rejected by the party leadership. Preobrazhenskii's economic formulas were solemnly condemned. The idea of developing heavy industry

at the expense of agriculture was rejected as a major danger
to the alliance between workers and peasants. The theory of
"primitive socialist accumulation"—patterned on Marx's
theories of the brutal exploitation and dispossession of small
landowners during the dawn of capitalism—was branded
heretical and a menace to the stability of the Soviet
regime.

Soon, however, the party radically changed its policy.
The reasons for this reversal were many. Among them may
be noted: the continuing political and economic isolation of
the country; a sharpening differentiation among the peasantry (leading to the strengthening of a rich peasant strat-
um); and finally increasing difficulty in persuading peasants
to market larger and larger amounts of grain in order to
maintain a high rate of industrialization and urbanization.
Taking over the policies of the defeated Left and emphasizing even more than before the need for heavy industry
and for autarkic development ("Socialism in One Country"),
the party leadership called for a massive investment effort
and for rapid industrialization as the *sine qua non* of Soviet
survival. Closing the debate on strategy and opening at the
end of 1928 the era of all-round planning, Stalin declared
in a famous attack against the Right that the party's policy
would henceforth "proceed from the premise that a fast rate
of development of industry in general and of the production
of the means of production in particular is the underlying
principle of, and the key to, the industrialization of the country, the underlying principle of, and the key to, the transformation of the entire national economy along the lines of
socialist development. But what does a fast rate of develop-

ment of industry involve?" asked Stalin; he answered, "It involves the maximum capital investment in industry."[21]

Thus sharply divergent orientations were debated by the Soviet Union's policy makers concerning the pace of the country's economic growth, the mobilization of its investible resources, and the pattern of its development. For Shanin, and for Bukharin and the Right, agriculture was the pacesetter for the growth of the economy as a whole; for Preobrazhenskii and the Left, and later for Stalin, heavy industry was the key. For the Right, the need for a sustained rate of capital formation in agriculture set definite limits to the transfer of its "surplus product" to industry. For the Left, the economy could be propelled into a phase of sustained high growth only if, during an initial critical period, substantial "surpluses" were extracted from agriculture for the development of basic industries.

Bukharin had conceded that certain transfers would have to be made from agriculture to industry, but he opposed the idea of manipulating industrial prices. Other economists, deeply concerned with the stability of the currency—Professor Katsenelenbaum for instance—suggested that industrialization be carried out exclusively through voluntary savings channeled through appropriate state credit institutions.[22] Katsenelenbaum rejected, as damaging to incentives to higher output in agriculture, the manipulation of industrial prices and the practices of high monopoly profits and high taxation. Preobrazhenskii advocated, on the contrary, the deliberate turning of the terms of trade in favor of industry—"unequal exchange" between agriculture and industry—up to the moment when a fully modernized industry would be able to turn out goods at prices lower than those on the world market. When, under Stalin, the leaders officially adopted the policy of "pumping over" capital accumulation from agriculture to industry, they solemnly promised not to increase prices of manufactured consumers' goods any further, but to decrease them as rationalization progressed in the state-industrial complex.[23] In practice, however, all producers' goods' prices were kept constant while consumers' goods' prices climbed steadily throughout the period of all-around planning. When price cuts were finally practiced, they affected only slightly the consequences of decades of inflation, and changed nothing at all in the underlying methods of taxation, which weighed heavily on the peasants both as producers and as consumers.[24]

Concerning the pattern of development, Shanin had advocated the traditional sequence, starting with agriculture and ending with heavy industry after light industry had grown sufficiently. Bukharin had switched about 1925 to the idea that heavy industry had to grow *pari passu* with light industry, in order to meet the peasant demand for agricultural machinery and consumer goods, while simultaneously preparing for the independence of the Soviet economy from the world market. The idea that industry and agriculture must develop simultaneously, the first at a slightly faster rate than the latter, was presented in 1926 as the "United States pattern of industrialization," the model to be followed by the USSR.[25] Other policy makers or economists—V. A. Bazarov for instance—advocated the development of light industries in order to cope with the immediate "real mass demand" of the peasant market, and of certain basic industries (like electricity) to supply the *potential* demand of the

economy.[26] Finally, Preobrazhenskii and the Left suggested
a complete departure from the idea of the concurrent expansion of a variety of industries, so planned that the pattern of
output would match the pattern of end-use—an idea stressed
by Bukharin in respect to strategy, and by Kondrat'ev and
others in respect to planning.[27] Preobrazhenskii and the
Left stressed instead the idea of systematic thrusts forward
by heavy industry, an idea interpreted subsequently by the
planners as positing the design of a more or less consistent
program around the "leading links" (the producers' goods
industries) and of open-end planning below the leading
links. The discarding of the simultaneous, balanced-develop-
ment approach in favor of vigorous thrusts forward by the
leading branches followed by the other branches and sectors at a variety of loosely planned paces of growth became
typical of Soviet strategy and planning.[28]

The acceptance of the idea of a continuous massive development effort in heavy industry determined a number
of other decisions, not only on the rate of capital formation
in the other sectors but also on the organizational set-up of
the economy as a whole and of agriculture in particular.
Preobrazhenskii had bluntly affirmed that a high rate of investment required the extraction of a large share of marketed
produce from agriculture by taxation and price manipulation,
and the eventual dispossessing of the small peasant. The
party had first rejected the theory of primitive socialist accumulation, but once it proceeded to extract a large share
of savings from agriculture, it had to carry out in practice
all of the other conclusions of Preobrazhenskii. The collectivization of the peasantry, started in 1929 and carried out

forcibly throughout the early 1930's, was instrumental in increasing the marketed share of agricultural produce. The peasant was compelled to deliver a crushing share of his produce at ridiculously low prices, while at the same time he lost control over his land.[29] The party's final strategy of development proceeded from the premises (a) that discontinuities existed on the supply side of savings and that large "surpluses" could be tapped by forcibly changing the structural set-up in agriculture; (b) that Soviet heavy industry could be "reconstructed" and shifted onto a high technological level without much concern for the demand of consumers in general or of the peasants in particular; and (c) that the "reconstruction" of industry would eventually change the technological conditions prevailing in agriculture, but that in respect to capital formation agriculture would have for a long time only a low priority.

The underlying principle of the NEP had been that the revival of industry was dependent on the revival of agricultural production. Preobrazhenskii and the Left suggested that this idea, sufficient for the period of recovery, was not satisfactory for the period of reconstruction. For the peasants' demand for consumers' goods one had to substitute the virtually unlimited demand for capital goods of the state and of its industry. The country was isolated; its capacity for survival in a world dominated by a different social system was uncertain; class differentiations within the peasantry represented a potential danger for the regime; there was doubt that the peasants would voluntarily market a sufficiently large proportion of their produce to advance the industrialization of the country to a significant extent. All these considerations finally pushed the "Center" of the party out of its "equilibrium" position, forced it to take over the theses of the "industrialists," and made it turn these theses into the regime's official strategy of development.

Notwithstanding a variety of changes in political climate and in organizational method, the tenets of this strategy have gone unchallenged in the USSR from Stalin to Khrushchev. It is doubtful whether they will be seriously challenged so long as the Soviet government continues to aim at reaching an unrivaled military and economic posture in the world.

The public at large rightly identifies the Soviet method of industrialization not with the emphasis upon heavy industry in general but with a set of specific options taken on the eve of the all-round planning era (opened in 1928) concerning certain key industrial branches—electricity, steel, and machine tools. One can hardly separate the Soviet strategy of development from these specific technological decisions. According to what criteria were these choices made? Originally, the logic of the situation of an isolated country shattered by the war, as well as careful observation of the basic technological trends in the most industrialized countries, guided the technological choices by Soviet policy makers and planners. Increasingly, however, the leaders' preferences centered on these intermediate products (steel, etc.) because they viewed them as the key ingredients of an autarkic industry and a high defense potential. As Soviet industrialization developed, new technological decisions had to be made by the Soviet engineers now operating at the technological frontier; however, at no time were the original decisions concerning energy, steel, and machine tools reexamined or treated as other than indispensable foundations of the whole Soviet strategy of economic growth.

Before the First World War a Communist leader and engineer by training, Gleb Krzhizhanovskii, had pointed out the key role played by electricity in the development of industrial Germany, and had suggested that Russia could solve its own agricultural problems and even "that of the world" if only it would develop extensively the use of electricity in agriculture.[30] The true importance of energy was, however, brought home to the Soviet leaders during the fuel crisis of 1920. Under the impact of the crisis and on the advice of Krzhizhanovskii,[31] Lenin seized in 1920 upon the idea of the importance of electricity and coined his famous slogan, "Communism is the power of the Soviets plus electricity."[32] The first Soviet plan, launched in 1920, concerned electricity: the so-called Plan GOELRO[33] was in fact the first Soviet long-term plan scheduling a vast construction program for an entire industrial branch. Though in practice this plan contributed only modestly toward Soviet recovery and toward the "reconstruction" of the economy as a whole, it has been glorified out of all proportion in Communist literature. The so-called "energy concept" of the economy—the idea of transforming all production functions throughout the economy and of securing large increases in output by means of electrification on a vast scale—became after 1920 an unquestioned article of Communist faith. The first decision of any Communist regime, from eastern Europe to China, has been in favor of raising the production of electricity. This is no longer a technological choice: it is a basic Communist belief.

It must be added, however, that an increased output of electricity does in time help the development of any economy launched on the path of industrialization.

The Soviet emphasis on power, steel, and machine building was an obvious and unavoidable choice for a shattered, isolated country, attempting its economic recovery on autarkic lines. It was a technological option which could be easily carried out in Russia thanks to the country's vast deposits of coal and iron. This option is, however, so well integrated into the "Soviet method of industrialization" that each and every Communist country, whether it has coal and iron or not, attempts to follow the same path of development with the same type of emphases. The east European countries have in effect dodged for a long time any serious cooperation in the field of metallurgy and machine construction: their policy makers have for many years stressed the idea that domestic production of electricity, steel, and machine tools is absolutely necessary to each country, no matter what its natural endowment may be. Even now the division of labor among these countries in metallurgy and machine tools remains limited.

As the Soviet economy has developed, numerous new technological decisions have had to be made. To the so-called energy concept of the economy, and to the emphasis on steel and machine tools, other choices were added. In the 1950's the idea of "chemization"—the introduction of chemical processes on a vast scale, notably in the petroleum, coal, and other industries—received a big build-up, as did the electrification idea during the 1920's. Furthermore, as the economy has developed, the wisdom of centering planning on key intermediate products, rather than on final demand, is

being increasingly questioned. But notwithstanding possible
and impending changes, the Soviet method of industrialization and planning remains, for the public at large, rooted in
the original technological options of the late 1920's.

4 Efficiency and the
Rate of Growth

WITH the establishment of the course toward autarky, industrialization, and preferential development of capital goods
industries in December 1925,[1] the Soviet policy makers and
planners raised a question which has since taken on an increasingly obsessional character not only for them but also
for a large part of humanity. The question is: how long will
it take the USSR to surpass the level of development of the
most advanced industrial countries?

The XVth Party Conference affirmed at the end of October
1926 that "all the efforts of the party and of the state" would
be directed toward this aim so as to reach it "in a minimal
historical period."[2] The goal of a maximum pace of growth
in capital accumulation and industrial output—a pace necessarily faster than in the United States—became the overriding goal of the Soviet strategy of development long before
the world's informed public opinion had seriously considered
either the magnitude of the Soviet challenge or the vastness
of the means being mobilized for its achievement. But if the
XVth Party Conference boldly asserted that the capitalist
rates of growth would certainly be surpassed thanks to the
"rational and planned utilization of all the resources avail-

able in the national economy," in fact policy makers and planners were sharply divided as to what methods to use for determining *a priori* the size of capital accumulation, the distribution of the investible resources, and the rate of growth in capital accumulation and output, in order to reach the posited goals in the shortest possible period.

A number of economists openly challenged the idea that the Soviet Union could or would match Russia's prewar rate of capital accumulation, maintain rates of output indefinitely at the levels attained during the NEP, or use efficiently all its investible resources. The most outstanding theoretician of the inevitable fall in accumulation and output rates was V. A. Bazarov. Assuming, first, that a socialist system could not keep consumption below the prewar tsarist level, Bazarov asserted that the USSR would for investment purposes dispose of a share of its income "not greater but rather smaller than a capitalist economy which is at the same level of development of its productive forces."[3] Stating that any recovery process takes the aspect of "a curve descending smoothly to the level of [the pre-disturbance] equilibrium," Bazarov pointed out that in such a process the rate of speed of growth in output necessarily "slackens as the difference diminishes between the given state of the system and the state of its stable [prewar] equilibrium."[4]

The idea of slackening rates of growth in both capital formation and output appeared under various other forms not only in the writing of Bazarov but also in the official planning documents released up to 1928. The assumptions concerning the fall in rates changed, however, significantly from one document to another. For example, the planning documents elaborated by a "Special Commission on the Reproduction of Fixed Capital"—which played a key role in the mid-1920's—embodied the idea of falling rates because, according to their authors, the initial all-out effort of accumulation required for launching the economy on the path of reconstruction could not and need not be matched subsequently by efforts of a similar intensity.[5] Other economists— Krzhizhanovskii, for instance—stressed that increasing rates of growth in capital formation might lead to decreasing growth rates in output, for a variety of reasons, notably the dispersion of investment on a wide front in order to keep in production plants of low efficiency, the sinking of large investment into long-term construction projects, etc.[6]

Split into various tendencies but united in their distrust of the "pessimists," most of the party's economists, of the left and center persuasions, rejected completely the theory of the "falling growth curve" and its underlying assumptions. The Left stressed that a high level of capital accumulation was attainable by shifting the "terms of trade" against the peasants. The Center asserted that a high accumulation was completely within the reach of the system even with price decreases in favor of the consumer, thanks to the extraordinary productive potentialities of socialist "planning and rationalization."

The party's economists next tackled the question of falling rates of output. A. Boiarskii pointed out that the processes of recovery and reconstruction interpenetrate each other so that no one could draw a fine line between them. However, thanks to massive introduction of new techniques, a qualitative "leap" occurs between the two processes as the economy is shifted onto a higher technological level where new and higher rates of output become possible.[7] Carried away by the idea of shifts in the pace of growth due to massive shifts in technology, certain party enthusiasts claimed that U.S. levels of industrial output could be reached and surpassed at a headlong pace. Fel'dman himself had affirmed that the "country had to think not only of the upper limits of industrialization, but also of its minimal rates," and defined these minimal rates as rates necessarily higher than those prevailing in the United States: "ten or at the maximum fifteen years is the period in whose course we must accomplish the reconstruction of all productive relationships in the economy."[8] At the end of 1929 a whole set of articles or pamphlets —by Zolotarev, Sabsovich, Kovalevskii—stressed the possibility and the necessity of very high rates of growth and promised the realization of "full communism" in less than ten years. According to Zolotarev there was no point in planning beyond 1936, since "beyond the second Five-Year Plan, during the transition to a mature communist economy . . . the concept of a plan will of course change in a radical way; it will grow into the planning of a classless society in which the functions of the state will begin to wither away."[9] Sabsovich asserted that planning should be based not on decelerating but on "gradually accelerating" rates of growth, since the introduction of new technology would necessarily lead to massive increases in productivity. He affirmed that "with respect to the scale of industrial production we shall considerably exceed, within fifteen years, the present level of development of the most advanced capitalist country, the USA, and leave far behind in eighteen to twenty years the level which it will be able to reach at that time, if it continues to develop under capitalist conditions."[10] Kovalevskii, who rejected Sabsovich's projected intersectoral relationships as conservative and his computations as too empirical, asserted, on the basis of generous assumptions of his own, that his sectoral projections guaranteed "the attainment of American consumption levels in ten years and a threefold increase over American consumption in fifteen years."[11]

Under the conflicting premises of the pessimists, who influenced the Right of the party, and of the "ultras," who reflected in an exaggerated way, particularly from 1928 on, the hopes of the leading bureaucracy engaged in the ruthless industrialization and collectivization drive, Gosplan steered a very uneasy course. Its approach to perspective planning was strictly empirical. On the basis of rough estimates of available physical resources and on the basis of some crucial technological options, the planners set "intuitively" the key targets for capacity and output of the priority branches— electricity, steel, and machine tools. From scheduled expansions and from sectoral and branch allocations, a sort of model of intersectoral relationships was constructed in physical terms. From these scheduled physical flows, national income and its division into accumulation and consumption was finally derived by the use of planned prices. The projected rates of growth in capacity and output of the leading branches were from the outset, and continued to remain, the determinants of the plan.[12]

The question remained: how to avoid a projection of these basic growth rates which would prove either too low (for time is of the essence) or too high (for the economy cannot be geared toward unachievable goals without terrific strains)? This is a problem for which the Soviet planners have not yet found the answer. The workers of Gosplan and of the Supreme Council of the National Economy, the leading organ of the state industry, were in the 1920's veering right and left according to the changing fortunes of the leading factions in the party's Central Committee. By 1927, when the Center under Stalin felt sufficiently strong to repudiate the Left and then to use the latter's own arguments for breaking the Right, the planners passed through a phase of feverish revaluation of the scheduled rates of growth included in their drafts of the first Five-Year Plan. The first draft of a five-year perspective plan drawn by Gosplan scheduled an increase in the gross value of output of industry by the end of the plan period of 67.9 per cent and 87.0 per cent in the minimum and maximum plan variants respectively. In its own draft, the Supreme Council of the National Economy proposed an increase of 97.6 per cent. Revising its assumptions and its estimates, Gosplan upped its targets by 1927 to 83.6 (minimum) or 98.7 per cent (maximum). After the XVth Party Congress in December 1927 the Supreme Council prepared a number of drafts in which the scheduled rates of growth of industrial output jumped from 108 to 122, 140, and finally to 167.7 per cent for the period 1927/28-1932/33. The Supreme Council's draft of August 1928 scheduled an increase of 141.7 per cent in the gross value of output of sector A (heavy industry) and of 109.6 for sector B (light industry). The December draft, which served in fact as the plan, scheduled an increase of 221 per cent for sector A and 130.3 per cent for B.[13] In theory, in 1932 group A increased by 290 per cent and group B by 163 per cent and "completion" of the plan was proclaimed a year ahead of schedule. While these official figures are questionable, since they were computed on the basis of doubtful weights,[14] it is nevertheless certain both that the over-all pace of development was extremely fast and that vast disruptions were caused in the economy as a whole by the unprecedented development of the heavy industry branches.

By 1932 Trotsky himself was warning from his exile against "adventurism" and was suggesting the need of a pause in the drive for industrialization.[15] The leading bureaucracy was not, however, ready to accept any suggestion which implied the need of a slowing down in the pace of development of the key industrial branches. It may be interesting to recall that in 1928 party optimists were forecasting a yearly growth rate of 26.3 per cent for group A and of 18.2 per cent for group B over the next three quinquennia. Officially, the growth rates for the first three long-term plan periods (the last interrupted in 1941) reached: for group A, 28.5, 19.0, and 15.0 per cent; for group B, 19.2, 17.1, and 13.2 per cent. Output growth rates did in fact follow, even in the distorted mirror of 1926-27 prices, a falling curve. The explanation may be due to the deep disruptions caused by the incredible forging ahead of the heavy industry branches, the progressive exhaustion of the advantages arising from economies of scale, full utilization of capacity, rationalization,[16] and finally, the fact that without regular increases in the productivity of capital a rising growth rate in output requires in turn a rising ratio of investment to total output[17]— while the share of capital accumulation in national income rose in real terms but perhaps not sufficiently over time.

When the great industrialization and collectivization drive got under way in 1929, most of the so-called "pessimists" advancing the theory of falling growth rates were tracked down by Stalin's secret police. Two infamous mass political trials—of the engineers and of the former Mensheviks—

at the beginning of the 1930's set the stage for the bloody purges of the middle and late 1930's. The engineers, who helped planning in its initial stages, and the former Menshevik or "bourgeois" statisticians and theoreticians, who helped formulate some of the most pertinent problems concerning planning theory and methodology—Groman, Bazarov, Kondrat'ev, Ginzburg, and many others—were first publicly humiliated, then condemned under trumped-up charges as "saboteurs" and "wreckers," and finally liquidated in Stalin's prisons.[18]

The top Soviet leaders believed that in order to attain their political and economic goals they alone must determine in detail the direction of the main processes of industrialization and the interconnections between them, that they alone must regulate the intensity of industrialization (and hence must set the level of capital accumulation), must decide on the extent and kind of capital construction, order the key outputs, play the role of innovator, and provide for the training and distribution of manpower. Hence, from the opening of the all-round planning era at the beginning of 1929, they concentrated vast administrative and operational powers in their own hands. The emphasis placed on strategic priorities, technological options, intuitive goal-setting, and mechanical balancing of key outputs, and an enormous number of directives from the top down toward the "planning front" as a whole, were deemed sufficient to insure the rapid and systematic growth of the economy in accordance with the leaders' political and economic goals and their attendant price policies. Cost-price considerations (in Marxian parlance, the operation of the "law of value") were not regarded as useful guides in the decisions of the central planners. The determination of a value yardstick to facilitate choices among different ways of producing future outputs was left to the discretion of engineering project makers and their designing bureaus. Finally, "profitability" (returns above cost) was established as a guiding principle (but not always as an automatic yardstick) for enterprises which since the early 1920's had been placed on a so-called autonomous business basis.

The Soviet leadership rejected the use of any normative principle in selecting among different types of future outputs. Deprived of any value yardstick and lacking both an integrated input-output balance of the economy and adequate information on the activities occurring in each branch and sector, the policy makers and planners concentrated their full attention on the expansion in output and capacity of a limited number of key intermediate producers' goods (steel, coal, metals, electricity) and of some basic consumers' goods (grains, fats, meat) and on their direct apportionment among processing industries. Tight control over intermediate products and their apportionment, plus price manipulations of various inputs, were designed to ensure, along with a second set of material and financial controls on the finished outputs themselves, that the operational managers would behave as the central planners wished them to—that is, that they would produce the desired output mix with the specific means provided for the purpose.

Their disregard of value considerations in central decisions, their apportionment of the main inputs, their reliance on a maze of often contradictory controls, and their use of price distortions did not mean that the central planners were indifferent to the problem of efficiency; they did not ignore the need to secure maximum returns in relation to the goals set by the policy makers. The truth is rather that the planners viewed efficiency as a narrow technological problem which could by and large be solved on technological grounds. In its planning directives to Gosplan, the XVth Party Congress ordered that "the plan of capital construction should aim at the most effective utilization of capital outlays," and that "yearly capital outlays must provide maximum investment in a number of comparatively basic new plants and of leading enterprises chosen for the reconstruction."[19] But the directives did not indicate how "the most effective utilization of capital outlays" could actually be measured.

With these cryptic orders in hand, Gosplan drew up its plans on the assumption of maximum effective utilization of available capacity and maximum utilization of present and potential resources, with attention to regional peculiarities and full employment, but with the aim of minimizing the absorption of labor in industry, using the most advanced technology, and reducing unit costs. Within this loosely defined framework it is hard to ascertain the actual criteria used by project makers and designers to choose among alternative processes, to decide between expansion of old plants and construction of new ones, to select among present and postponable outlays, etc. What is clear, however, is that a well-nourished discussion developed around these problems in the late twenties but did not yield either a satisfactory theoretical formulation or a yardstick acceptable to the party's leadership.

The trouble with this discussion in the 1920's—and with various Soviet discussions since then in the same field—is that many of the participants confused the question of (a) fixing the final output mix, and the capital allocation for the purpose (these decisions were made by the central planners) with that of (b) choosing among alternative ways of producing this final output mix within the limits of the specified allocations of capital. Those who got involved in the question of determining the structure of output and the pattern of capital allocation raised again a question that had been answered during the debate on the strategy of development and its specific pattern of priorities. Such persons searched for criteria of "effectiveness" by relating changes in output to increments of capital (or of both capital and labor), and thus raised the problem of the utilization of capital. Those who, on the other hand, eliminated the question of output from their calculations altogether, and who attempted to relate investments to savings in cost, deliberately reduced their search for effectiveness to a choice among processes— a choice in capital *intensity,* not in capital *allocation*—for producting a predetermined output mix.

Among those who raised anew the question of the over-all strategy of development itself a typical example is N. A. Kovalevskii, to whom we have already referred.[20] His suggestions for drawing up a general plan, following Fel'dman's schemata, were rejected because he proposed that value relationships, and not physical output targets, be taken as the starting points of a perspective plan; because he further affirmed that certain interconnections necessarily prevailed among value categories; and finally, because he advised that capital-output ratios be used to rationalize the planner's choices among alternative patterns of investment. From the debates on Kovalevskii's proposals at the Communist Academy one gets a revealing glimpse of the official approach to value indicators and of the planning techniques prevailing in the late 1920's. "The economic meaning of the concept of effectiveness is very vague," says A. I. Petrov. "We should plan labor productivity on the basis of technical calculations in various specific sectors of the economy. Once we have obtained this expected growth of productivity we should then fix the division of national income into parts to be consumed and to be accumulated."[21] "Kovalevskii considers only the productive forces, without any regard to our economic policy," adds R. E. Vaisberg.[22] "It is very curious," stresses A. Kon, "that at the basis of all the constructs of comrade Kovalevskii there is a certain coefficient, the coefficient of effectiveness." After affirming that this coefficient is both "illegitimate and irrelevant," Kon adds: "We are not concerned with the ratio of net output to expended labor, but with net output and capital funds which embody technology, in all its varieties, as well as live labor."[23] Only the central planners, on the basis of established strategy, can determine both the level of the key output targets and the means—i.e., the capital allocation and the technology—with which to produce them. This is a point on which the Soviet policy makers have never accepted compromises.

Any attempt to use profit as a criterion for determining the pattern of industrialization, even below the level of "top planning decisions," was looked upon very suspiciously. This was the case with the suggestions of N. N. Shaposhnikov and R. Gol'dberg, who emphasized the importance of profitability at the enterprise level. After affirming, tongue in cheek, that once one accepts the idea of autarky, it is certainly "better to have a state industry that is more costly and less effi-

cient than foreign private industry, than to have no industry
at all," Shaposhnikov asserted that from this "theoretical
point of view" no one could oppose the domestic development of any specific new industrial branch or give a categor-
ical answer to the question if "one should rather have [first]
the Volga-Don Canal and [then] Dnieprostroi, or the other
way around." But, added Shaposhnikov, economic science
does establish a criterion which if considered will not interfere with economic policy. This criterion is: "the more profit-
able any enterprise is, the more beneficial for the commu-
nity."[24] Gol'dberg pointed out that within the Soviet economy
"profits are being assessed every day and everywhere by
the most haphazard, antediluvian and home-made methods" and that a precise criterion of profitability was indispensable. This criterion, affirmed Gol'dberg (generalizing the
Cobb-Douglas type of analysis applied in the United States
for the period 1899-1922) is the ratio of change in output to
the increments in capital and wage bill. Efficiency, according
to Gol'dberg, will improve when the rate of increase in capital per worker is smaller than the reduction in number of
workers (and in the total wage bill), with output staying
the same.[25]

Other economists—S. Rozentul, for example—tried to provide a sophisticated synthetic formula which would take into
account not only the efficiency achieved on the level of enterprises "as measured by the increase in their profitability"
but also other secondary effects, such as benefits obtained by
the labor force, the increment in income received from "nonproductive" expenditures (services), etc.[26] L. Iushkov finally
noted that a "norm" of effectiveness could be derived for the
economy as a whole from (a) the centrally scheduled targets

and the centrally scheduled volume of capital investments and pattern of allocations by branches, and (b) the capital-output ratios resulting from the various alternatives tentatively selected at the level of enterprises. Once the "limit of effectiveness" was found at which all contemplated investment would be absorbed, the final choice among alternatives would, at each level, be made in relation to this norm, taken as a sort of "objective" rate of return. Only the projects with ratios above the norm would be implemented, with preference for the alternative with the highest returns.[27]

But if the state leadership was stressing the idea of profitability at the level of the state-owned, autonomously managed state enterprises, it was not at all eager to depart from its haphazard home-made methods of assessing profitability, or to take profitability into account at the higher planning level for the allocation of resources. "Profitability" was to remain only a yardstick for checking the performance of enterprises in relation to the goals set, not a criterion for setting these goals.

Departing from output coefficients, Ia. Rozenfel'd and G. Abezgauz showed how the managers were in practice getting around the question of the relationship between profitability and investment: they simply ignored it, and related each investment to reductions in cost. Ia. Rozenfel'd indicated that, in the choice among alternative ways of producing a given output, the "arbitrator" could be the ratio of investment to cost savings per unit, times producible units during the estimated life of the asset.[28] Abezgauz affirmed that what mattered was the pace at which the "pay-back" of investments was achieved through savings in cost. Since both investment outlays and recoupments vary from year to year and asset to asset, the choice among alternatives should be made by taking into account the specific pay-backs over a period of perhaps ten years (i.e., of two perspective plans), with preference for the project with the highest pay-back percentage.[29] This shift in focus from problems of capital allocation to those of capital intensity did not, however, satisfy the leading bureaucracy for many years, and the official fog on the question of "efficiency" remained dense for decades.

Denying that any single criterion could be selected to help either the planner in allocating capital or the project maker in choosing among alternative processes, some economists suggested that planning and project making were, in the given Soviet conditions, necessarily "eclectic" in their choice of criteria. Rejecting specifically Abezgauz' approach, M. Barun asserted that any capital outlay had a lot of "different effects" (concerning location, technology, scale, organization of production) in either a private or a centrally run economy.[30] Professor L. N. Litoshenko, who by that time was severely pulled between the need of toning down his critique of the planners and his own standards of professional integrity, noted that in a monetary-commercial system—be it capitalist or socialist—the same criterion (profit) should in principle prevail in respect to capital allocation; but, since none of the conditions which make profitability meaningful exist under socialism—especially mobility of capital among branches, and rational prices—the planners, as the Gosplan's texts demonstrate, must resort to a whole set of criteria, e.g., the needs of various branches assessed by the balancing method, closeness of raw material, obsolescence of existing equipment, etc. The result, Litoshenko pointed out, may per-

haps appear adequate for each specific case; but freedom
to combine the various criteria in a number of ways excludes
the possibility of ascertaining whether the plan which finally
emerges is really the best plan.[31]

The lack of any acceptable criteria of choice led in practice, as Krzhizhanovskii himself noted by the beginning of
1929, to insoluble conflicts between the objective of full
employment and the drive to rationalize production "at all
costs;" between the aim of introducing the highest technology and the need to keep obsolete plants in production in
order to meet the prescribed goals; between the possibility
of borrowing the most advanced technology and the lack of
investible resources and skilled labor for using them; between the drive to increase production quickly and the tying
down of large investments in long-term projects.[32]

The decision to draw up the plan on the basis of physical
flows and the deliberate distortion of cost-price relationships
rendered impossible, within the Soviet planning framework,
a solution of the question of rational allocation of resources.
How, then, can one account for the impressive growth of
the Soviet system notwithstanding the wastage of resources
in relation to the planners' goals? The achievement of high
levels of capital accumulation by direct allocation of basic
intermediate products, such as steel, at the place of production; the allocation of physical resources to the key branches
in the quantities and qualities desired; the concentration of
efforts integrally and sequentially according to priorities
from the first to the next down the line; the introduction of
the most advanced technology for the main processes in the
leading branches; the continuous prodding of operational
management and labor to keep them in line—all these con-

tributed to achieving the high defense and industrialization objectives set for the USSR by its Communist leadership. These are typical "war economy" methods; the uniqueness of the Soviet experience consists in the fact that they have never been applied on such a vast scale and for such a long time anywhere else.

The goal set in the 1920's, to reach and surpass in fifteen years the United States' industrial capacity, industrial output, or standard of living appears incredibly unrealistic today. The United States' growth has far exceeded Soviet expectations, while Soviet growth has fallen below Soviet forecasts. The critical "fifteen years" is still presented as the period necessary to overtake the United States, but today, after decades of intensive industrialization, this goal projects heavy shadows on the late 1960's and early 1970's.[33]

5 Principles and Procedures
of Planning

THE Marxists dismiss the classical economic doctrine that stresses the self-regulating capacities of the market. From this basic and arbitrary postulate a number of crucial consequences flow both in Marxian economic theory and in Soviet planning. The "fundamental contradiction" of capitalism is alleged to consist in the opposition between "socialized" organization in the individual factory and "social anarchy in the production as a whole." While, writes Engels, capitalist factory production depends on "division of labor, upon a definite plan," production in capitalist society at large is "ruled by absence of plan, by accident, by anarchy."[1] Since the market is anarchic, Engels and Lenin assert further that transitions from perfect competition to monopoly and oligopoly are attempts to limit economic "planlessness" and, therefore, steps toward integral planning—which, however, socialism alone can install.[2] Thus planning, according to Marxist theory, is the opposite of market regulation of production, and, paradoxically, monopoly and oligopoly are steps toward full-fledged planning. By definition, therefore, in this theoretical framework the socialist economy is a non-market economy with a centrally planned organization and regulation of production.

Comprehensive planning evidently requires extensive and methodical coordination among current economic activities and those which will arise in the future as various branches and sectors expand at different rates of growth. This coordination requires, in turn, the establishment of a number of plans: short-term operational plans and long-term "perspective" or general plans, that is, expansion plans covering a number of years and at least certain key industries and sectors. Furthermore, operational and expansion plans must be differentiated and coordinated at various organizational levels, such as the industry, branch, sector, and region.

How can these plans be drawn in a realistic manner and how can they be made to mesh with one another at various points in time? Must all current activities be coordinated? Must scheduled patterns of output and of end-use match perfectly? To what extent must the plan be shaped by past trends, and to what extent and in what ways can the policy maker and the planner aim at changing prevailing interrelationships between branches and sectors? Is the planner's freedom of choice of goals equal in respect to all sectors and to all time periods? How can the planner achieve consistency among all his goals and efficiency in the use of resources while dispensing increasingly with market relations and market mechanisms?

These problems began to confront the Soviet policy makers and planners on the morrow of the Bolshevik revolution of 1917, as the leaders stressed the need of an integrated national plan for all the economic activities of the country.

But a single integrated national plan came into being only in 1929, eleven years after the revolution.

The period 1917-1928 is often described in Soviet official literature as the period of the "struggle for the plan."[3] The "struggle," according to these sources, involved not only the formulation and selection of workable planning principles and procedures, but also the preparation of the so-called "objective" conditions for planning, that is, in Soviet theory and practice, the systematic limitation of the scope of certain types of market relations. The search for planning principles broadened and intensified the debate between "voluntarists" and "determinists." The search for planning procedures put to an acid test the alleged opposition between planned order and market anarchy, and raised the question of the respective limits of centralization and decentralization. The preparation of the "objective" conditions for planning raised a host of crucial problems concerning the policy makers' strategy of development, the pace of sectoral growth, the interaction among different systems of ownership and production in the Soviet economy, and finally, the question of the possible place of "atomistic" (individualistic) agriculture in the framework of planning.

In the Soviet pattern of development large-scale nationalization, and a high centralization of both administrative and operational managerial functions—that is, a wide use of centralized commands to determine investment and all aspects of current output[4]—were all viewed as normal steps toward integral planning and were all associated with the early phase of the Bolshevik regime, the period of so-called War Communism. When the Bolsheviks launched the New

Economic Policy (NEP) in the spring of 1921, deliberately restoring market relationships on a wide scale, they limited the sphere of centralized operational commands in the state sectors and in the economy as a whole, and at the same time they gave up for the time being the idea of extensive planning. High centralization at all operational levels was so deeply interwoven with planning that the latter appeared necessarily impaired when the former had to be limited. Bolsheviks of Left or Right persuasion advocated or rejected planning according to their attitude toward market relations —that is, toward the NEP—and toward industry and privately owned agriculture—that is, toward the regime's over-all strategy of development and toward its nationalization and collectivization policies. For no one doubted then that over-all planning necessarily meant both the liquidation of market relationships and the return to a system of highly centralized administration. Those who had an increasing distaste for the consequences of the NEP, and who stressed in particular the danger of socio-economic differentiation among the peasants, became the earliest and most persistent advocates of all-embracing planning. Those who affirmed that recovery and future growth depended upon the conservation of market relationships and upon peasant agriculture ranged themselves against any extensive planning. When the NEP was brought to a close and over-all planning started, the sphere of market relations shrank, that of administrative commands expanded, and agriculture as a whole was engulfed in a massive process of collectivization.

In order better to grasp the various positions taken in the debate on planning, we shall try to disentangle the discussions on planning *principles* from those on planning *procedures*. The voluntarists, who were called "teleologists" in the planning debates,[5] stressed the need for a national plan based on a number of key targets for the priority branches, toward whose fulfillment the economy as a whole should be geared. The plan, they said, must not be merely a summary of individual branch plans; it should be a set of national goals binding the economy in its entirety and dominating current operations and the expansion plans of each branch and sector, according to a scale of priorities reflecting the regime's over-all strategy of development. All efforts should be directed toward implementing the push forward of the priority branches. The teleologists affirmed that planning is a conscious act and that there can be no talk of planning until the policy makers have set goals and given directives. By definition, the plan is not a piece of neutral research into past trends and their mechanical extrapolation; it is a purposive act setting specific assignments which embody the policy makers' will to change prevailing social and economic relationships. Consequently, the over-all aims of the policy makers will establish the basic premises of the plan.[6]

There are thus objective limits on the freedom of choice enjoyed by policy makers and planners, but these limits are neither rigid nor immutable. As one of the chief representatives of this tendency, S. G. Strumilin, put it, the further away in time the goals are placed, the greater are the opportunities for the free play of the "social organizer's" creative ideas. The opportunities are vast in a general plan period of fifteen to twenty years; they are more restricted in an intermediate, perspective plan period of, say, five to seven years; they are almost negligible in a yearly plan period. In

the longer perspective, directives or prescriptions predominate; in the shorter run "prognoses" or forecasts based on
past trends necessarily hold sway.[7]

After stressing the primacy of goals in perspective planning, the teleologists contended further that planning, being "social engineering," necessarily displaces and recreates
relationships among branches and sectors. The crucial
changes planned for the leading branches of the economy
have to be carried out, no matter what stresses and strains
they may provoke in the rest of the economy. In the process of massive shuffling of socio-economic parameters, bottlenecks and disequilibria of all kinds are unavoidable.
"Change," wrote an official proponent of this policy, "cannot take place smoothly like driving on a well-paved high-
way from one state of equilibrium to another."[8]

The teleologists, who advocated designing a consistent
"core" plan for the leading branches and open-end planning
for the rest of the economy, and after them the party's leadership, came to combat with tooth and nail the idea of general
equilibrium, as if the latter implied immutable relationships
among economic variables and particularly among the
growth rates of sectors and of systems of ownership. The
term "equilibrium" was construed as a cover-up for the idea
of unavoidable "automaticity" of economic processes and
of their coordination through the market, while planned
"balance"—i.e., the deliberate establishment of new patterns
of sectoral interdependence around the "key" branches—was
affirmed to be its opposite. These involved distinctions between "equilibrium" and "balance" still plague Soviet planning literature. What was really hidden behind the attack on
"equilibrium"—that is, the attack on the comprehensive bal-

ancing of output and end-uses—was on the one hand a fight against certain tendencies in the party, and on the other a justification of the stresses and strains that would inevitably result from the thrusts forward of the leading branches and the high-handed planning methods of the Soviet bureaucrats.

In agreement with both their concepts of purposive change and their industrialist strategy, the teleologists suggested that the starting points of any Soviet plan are the targets set for the "basic" industries, and that the "core" of any Soviet plan is the input-output balances of these basic industries. But the planner's information is always imperfect, and no plan can take into account all the variables involved at each point in time. Moreover, new possibilities become apparent or unexpected bottlenecks arise as the plan unfolds. Hence the Soviet planners affirmed that they could and must intervene at any moment and at any level of the organizational set-up; they must continuously direct and control the detailed implementation of the plan from the center of command.[9] Thus, along with the idea of the primacy of the top priority goals and the unavoidability of disproportions, the teleologists stressed also the idea of the need of elbow room —"maneuverability"—for the policy maker and planner as the plan unfolds.

The second school of thought, that of the "geneticists," stressed the crucial significance if not the absolute necessity of objective, deterministic processes in the shaping of social economic changes and in the formulation of any plans. Writing in the early years of the NEP, V. G. Groman affirmed that, in contrast to utopianism, "scientific socialism" underlined the idea that "the genetic development of society must create the forces capable of securing both the power and the will to transform society in a certain direction," and that consequently "the method and the forms of such transformation are dictated by the objective conditions of society and the hidden objective tendencies of its development."[10] Groman contended that the direction of change was predetermined and that the planner's freedom to allocate resources in new ways was sharply limited. In short, the objective conditions set the premises of the plan.

In a less metaphysical form, the economist Kondrat'ev remarked that the planner's goals, at no matter what point in the future, are in the final analysis only forecasts based on a number of assumptions which may or may not turn out to be correct. The real problem for him was to submit the planner's goals to the test of some general criteria, such as efficiency in the scheduled use of resources.[11] Another "geneticist," V. A. Bazarov, advanced a somewhat different thesis: that the planner's freedom of choice varies greatly in practice from one economic sector to another. In industry, where specific forms of organization and interchange prevail, the plan can consist of a set of directives. But in agriculture, where a number of "planless" elements predominate— atomistic organization, market relations, the weather, etc.— the plan can take only the form of a forecast. Consequently, suggested Bazarov, the plan must be not only a genetic inquiry but also a teleological construct, the respective spheres of forecasts and directives being determined primarily by the existence or absence of market forces. The task of the planner will consist in blending adroitly "the genetic and teleological methods in the search for the optimum course of development."[12]

Next, stressed the geneticists, the economy must be viewed

as a harmonious, organic whole—as Bazarov put it, "a maxi-
mally stable system of mobile equilibrium." This posits the
need of achieving "internal consistency of the separate elements of the reconstruction process,"[13] that is, the need of
"setting goals consistent among themselves," and achieving
balanced growth. In order to avoid any violation of the principle of proportional development of the different elements
of the economy which mutually determine one another, Groman suggested that the planner must study the basic regularities existing in the economy and construct his plan—in fact
his projections—by taking them into strict account.[14] Not
only the former Mensheviks Groman and Bazarov but also
the Bolshevik N. I. Bukharin underlined the internal unity
of Soviet society—no matter how contradictory this unity
might be—and demanded that the planner start planning
from a model of the basic relationships among sectors of the
economy, a model analogous to Marx's schema of simple and
enlarged reproduction.[15] All the geneticists, no matter what
their nuances, stressed the need of not losing sight of the
organic unity of the economy, even though they conceded
that in practice any plan would have an unfinished, relative
character, because of the unavoidable impact on it of "planless" (market-determined) elements. Finally, and this is important, former Mensheviks and even Right-wing Bolsheviks
suggested, in conformity with their over-all strategy of development, that the planner should start his planning from
forecasts of consumers' demand, rather than from targets
for producers' goods, since they held that economic growth
and the rise of living standards are indissolubly connected.

These were the general principles which teleologists and
geneticists respectively formulated as they tried to solve the

problem of devising planning techniques and methods of execution. Rejecting the need of any macro-model relating in specific ways the crucial variables of the economy, or any preliminary balance of the economy as a whole, and deriding the idea of full consistency among planned goals, and the idea of balanced growth, the teleologists affirmed that planning is as much an art as a science, that absolute consistency is not of this world, and that what matters in a process of development is to determine what sectors of the economy should be singled out for rapid growth. Any plan, said Strumilin, is only an approximation, not necessarily the best one. The construction of plans, like the more elementary art of building, is a kind of engineering, and in social engineering, as in any other type of engineering, a problem can be solved in any number of ways: "no one solution is the only one possible, absolutely accurate, and unquestionably optimal."[16] Citing the example of the old masters who had built at a higher cost and a slower pace than would be necessary today such marvels as the Greek Acropolis or the French Notre Dame, Strumilin noted that these architects accomplished their purpose even though they had to allow "a far larger factor of safety in their designing than the theory of strength of materials would have required of them."[17]

Having thus rejected for practical purposes "the accuracy to which science pretends," and having reaffirmed the need of elbow room in planning, Strumilin noted that a perspective plan can be viewed in practice as an interrelated program built around a core of engineering blueprints drawn for a number of well-selected branches of industry and coordinated on the basis of given time sequences. First, the scale of development of each key branch is planned according to the policy makers' goals, and the available and potential resources are roughly assessed. Then the blueprints are integrated into a sort of approximate model of the future, always attempting to adjust each of the succeeding plans to the preceding ones. The key programs determine all the others; the planning sequence goes from basic producers' goods—intermediate products such as steel, other metals, electricity, etc.—to industry as a whole, then to all other sectors, with agriculture last.

Starting from a general expansion plan covering ten to fifteen years, coordinating a number of basic engineering blueprints, the planner concretizes his intermediate and short-run objectives in an increasingly complex way as he moves down from the general to the perspective and the yearly working plan, and from the planning center to the level of execution. Both the concretization of the plans and their harmonization at various organizational levels are done by successive approximations—a method which circumvents the absence of a basic macro-economic model.

In principle, the perspective plan should be embodied in two variants—minimum and maximum—and should be redrawn each year in the light of the past year's achievements. The variants would set "boundaries" in the execution of the plan: falling short of the minimum would indicate the danger of maladjustments ahead; reaching the maximum would represent top performance of the economy, since these series would be constructed upon the most favorable assumptions (no harvest failures, availability of foreign loans, etc.). The variants would serve as guidelines to the yearly, quarterly, and other working plans, while these in turn would serve as correcting factors for the perspective plan.

Decisions on capital construction for the key branches would determine the dynamics of plans for all other sectors. In turn, operational goals established in physical terms, on the basis of physical balances of resources and their allocation, and on the basis of capital construction commissioned, would be determined for the leading producers' goods industries, then for industry as a whole, then for the other sectors. The goals for agriculture—expansion, patterns of output, marketed share—would follow the plans for industry. All these goals would form a system of assignments: they would be specific and realistic within the framework chosen and would conform to present and estimated resources. While the goals would be binding for all, the central planner would not view them as immutable: he would adjust them as the program itself unfolded or as the policy maker decided to shift some of his objectives.[18]

The "geneticists," as well as a number of economists who were not necessarily in full agreement with all their theses, rejected the teleologist approaches to planning as non-scientific improvisation, and accused the teleologists of substituting intuition for the serious search for optimality, consistency, and efficiency in planning. The economists N. D. Kondrat'ev and G. A. Fel'dman, for example, pointed out that successive approximations cannot be considered as a "method" of determining and coordinating economic goals. They offer only a "technique" which, said Kondrat'ev, helps to harmonize a number of branch or sectoral balances of resources and allocations but does not help to establish the goals toward which these allocations aim nor explain how these goals have been selected.[19] Fel'dman noted that a broad knowledge of "the general laws of Marx" is not sufficient equipment for planning. What is required is "a consistent system of equations to determine the natural dynamic relationships between the basic elements of the economy." Once such a system of core formulas is established, the "technique of successive approximations" may be a useful supplement, but to use the latter in the absence of the former is to turn planning "'either into guessing or into the Sisyphean labor of a genius builder who substitutes intuition for a system."[20]

What was meant by "intuition" may be illustrated by the following incident, which occurred during a discussion of one of N. A. Kovalevskii's reports at the Communist Academy in 1930. It concerned the selection by Gosplan of the goal of an output of ten million tons of pig iron for the Soviet economy. Answering his critics, who were clamoring that this goal was far too low and had been arrived at on the basis of simple extrapolation of past trends, Kovalevskii remarked: "Anyone who has anything at all to do with planning, and with the Five-Year Plan in particular, knows that the goal of ten million tons of pig iron output was one of the main points of a terrific controversy. Those who started from the growth tendencies of the metal industry maintained that we could not produce more than four to six million tons of steel as a *maximum maximorum*. Only the iron will of the party and of the working class, seizing intuitively upon the future development possibilities of the economy and basing this foresight particularly on consciousness of the advantages of our system, put through this task, which exceeds twice what appeared to be the limit on the basis of the possibilities of growth of a given branch."[21]

Having rejected the procedure of drawing up a balance of expansion and one of output and allocation separately for each branch, with each goal derived intuitively or by some form of expertise, Kondrat'ev, Fel'dman, and a number of other economists pointed out that the linking of these balances by successive approximations could not in any way insure that the resulting integrated economic model would be optimal or even achievable. Many such projections could be constructed, as Strumilin himself pointed out. But unlike the engineer, who need not solve the problem of whether his building materials or monetary resources will be available, the planner must make sure that scheduled resources included in his projections will be effectively available at the time, and in the magnitude and specifications required by the plans. The planner must not only provide an abstract optimal solution; he must also make sure of its workability— that is, he must assess correctly the type and nature of the restraints under which he is going to operate.[22]

What is implied by workability may perhaps be illustrated by the following remark of N. I. Bukharin. After pointing out in a discussion on 1927 performance that industry had developed at "a frantic pace," generating a frantic demand for intermediate products and creating innumerable bottlenecks, Bukharin noted: "if there is no brick and if its production in a given season cannot (for technical reasons) go beyond a set magnitude, then one may not frame construction programs which exceed that limit and thereby cause a demand which cannot be covered, since no matter how much you go on forcing the pace of construction, you still will not make factory buildings and dwellings out of thin air."[23] Deriding Strumilin's proposal to turn planning into an art, M. Birbraer noted that Strumilin's examples of the masterful successes of the architects of the Acropolis or of Notre Dame are not too convincing, "particularly because there were many unfortunate examples in history—many more than that certain number of fortunate ones to which Strumilin refers—of constructions without scientific foundations which crumbled away long before their elevation was completed."[24]

Among the proposals for putting planning on an analytical basis, a special place must be reserved here for the brilliant suggestion made by M. Barengol'ts—to which we have already alluded—concerning the utilization of technical coefficients. Working along the lines suggested by Popov and Litoshenko in their "Balance of the National Economy," Barengol'ts pointed out that on the assumption of stable technological conditions "the coefficients of interindustry turnover relative to the so-called gross turnover"—i.e., the ratios of inputs to gross output—"will provide in physical terms (and, with a correction for price fluctuation, in value terms) fairly stable dynamic indicators to determine the total volume of consumption and of interindustry turnover as well as to establish the specific relations among various industries."[25] But the use of such "invariant" building blocks for determining in a consistent way the "volume of consumption and of interindustry turnover" at various levels of output was apparently not resorted to either in the Supreme Council of the National Economy or in Gosplan, though many other experiments of an input-output type were carried out at the time in the planning agencies.[26]

Another outstanding analytical proposal is the one formulated by G. A. Fel'dman which we have already discussed at some length.[27] Let us recall here only that Fel'dman aimed specifically at constructing a model on which the plan "in its abstract form" could be based, and with the help of which a set of variants could be drawn. Using essentially Fel'dman's method, N. A. Kovalevskii attempted to construct a so-called "working hypothesis" of the general plan. His schema and its underlying assumptions were, however, sternly criticized, since, as we saw, they posited the existence of objective criteria for guiding planners' choices in the allocation of investment, a fact which implicitly put into question the over-all strategy of development and its specific emphases. The party leadership and its economists rejected all analytical proposals in planning and the main ideas which they implied, namely, planning backward from forecasted final demand, and matching scheduled outputs with end-uses. They continued instead to stress the idea of planning from the "producers'" goods side—i.e., setting targets for the output of producers' goods and constructing "core" balances to coordinate input and output in producers' goods industries—and to execute their plans by means of methodical pressure for the fulfillment and overfulfillment of these goals without too much concern for the stresses and strains provoked in the rest of the economy.

Besides the official obsession with accelerating the growth in productive capacity and thrusting forward on the key military and producers' goods branches, a number of factors facilitated the triumph of pragmatism in planning. Significant among these were the domineering traditions of the leading bureaucracy and its lack of economic sophistication, the absence of experienced planners and of educated managerial "cadres," and the abysmally low standards of statistical information in industry and even in other fields.[28]

The first expansion plan for a whole industrial branch was drawn and approved in 1920. This plan, the Plan GOELRO, concerned, as we have stated,[29] electricity only, but has often been described erroneously as the first Soviet general or perspective plan. At the time, the IXth Congress of the party (March 29-April 5, 1920) proclaimed the need of coordinating the activity of the economy on the basis of a single plan—an idea then stressed by Trotsky and derided by one of the future leaders of the Right, Rykov;[30] but as we have said, the turn toward the NEP pushed the idea of an over-all national plan into the background. When a State Planning Committee (Gosplan) was finally established in the Council of Labor and Defense, in April 1921, as successor and continuator of the GOELRO commission, it had no powers whatever, and consisted of a meager staff of only forty persons. Its organization was directed toward dealing with current planning problems not exceeding one year, since in the conditions of the time "the preparation of more concrete projects (other than the one on electrification) for a whole series of years ahead appeared too abstract and too academic."[31]

Gosplan focused initially on relatively minor, episodic problems, and its reports dealt with such questions as "Special measures regarding the fuel supply of the republic," "Aid to the southeastern region, stricken with poor crop," "Regulation of the movement of refugees in poor regions," "The sowing of winter crops in 1921 in those localities of the RSFSR which suffered from poor crops," "The collapse of bridges in Novo Balitsa, Bykov, and Shilovka."[32] Perspective planning was at that early time attempted in a rudimentary way in various People's Commissariats, usually at the level of the Republics. Gosplan itself was not enabled to examine such drafts until the summer of 1923. From then on a large part of Gosplan's efforts was turned toward perspective planning. In the last quarter of 1923 Gosplan took up the discussion of the first plan of a major industrial branch submitted to it—the "Five-Year Plan for the Metal Industry, 1923/24-1927/28,"—compiled in the industry's Central Administration by the engineers Khrennikov and Gartvan. Soon afterward, Gosplan discussed a comprehensive draft covering the whole of the so-called "census" industry and its thirty-two branches—the "Industrial Five-Year Plan for 1923/24-1927/-28," prepared by the engineer Kalinnikov. The following year Gosplan considered a whole range of branch plans, notably a Five-Year Plan for Transportation drawn by engineer Neopikhanov, and a Five-Year Plan for Agriculture drawn in the Commissariat of Agriculture by Professor Kondrat'ev. A year later, attempts were finally made, both inside and outside Gosplan, to pass from branch planning to the formulation of a single plan for the economy as a whole.

A powerful impulse in this direction was given by the establishment at the Presidium of the Supreme Council of the National Economy, in March 1925, of a "Special Commission on the Reproduction of Fixed Capital" (OSVOK).[33] The commission, which grew into a major planning organization under the direction of Piatakov, and which undertook the preparation of a five-year industrial plan, released before its dissolution in September 1926 a total of twenty-nine detailed drafts ("hypotheses") for the output and equipment of various industries for the period 1925/26-1929/30.[34] Another special commission succeeded it, also at the Presidium of the Supreme Council of the National Economy, under the direction of A. M. Ginzburg, with the task of drafting a single national Five-Year Plan on the foundations laid by OSVOK. This commission released a year later a comprehensive volume of *Materials on a Five-Year Plan for the Economy of the USSR 1926/27-1930/31*, but never published a final plan.[35]

Meanwhile Gosplan, which had also grown from a committee of forty statisticians to a powerful organization with over a thousand specialists, released in 1925 its first one-year plan for the economy as a whole—the so-called Control Figures for 1925/26—and made known soon afterward its first rough draft of a five-year perspective plan. The publication of the Control Figures was greeted as a major event by the "industrialists," who saw in it a decisive step toward comprehensive planning and, implicitly, the end of the NEP. Though Trotsky thought to discern in the rows of Gosplan's numbers the "socialist music of the future," and though this publication did indeed underline the trend toward planning, the Control Figures were only a timid beginning. They did not formulate any new policy or new tasks, and were subsequently proved incorrect by the country's performance during the indicated year.[36] The Control Figures for 1925/26 were followed by yearly Control Figures up to the end of the 1920's.

Gosplan's first rough draft of a five-year plan, for 1925/26-1929/30, was presented at the meeting of its agencies in March 1926. Its second, more elaborate, draft of a five-year plan, for 1926/27-1930/31, was presented at the meeting of the same agencies in March 1927. A third, more complete, draft for 1931/32 was fully worked out by the autumn of 1929, when the XVth Congress of the All-Union Communist Party published its extensive "Directives" for the formulation of the first Five-Year Plan. The directives expressed officially the adoption of the strategy of rapid expansion of capacity in the leading branches as the fundamental line of the party, and stressed also that planning on a large scale had become possible because the state industrial complex had become increasingly independent of market forces ("market anarchy"), which allegedly had handicapped planning in the past.

When national planning came to the Soviet scene, it came as the servant of a specific strategy and as a substitute for the "spontaneous," "anarchic" play of the market. The idea that the sphere of centralized management and planning could expand or contract, that directives from above and the market mechanism could be fruitfully combined even in the sphere of interindustry relations, largely escaped the Soviet policy makers of the late twenties. Planning of interindustry flows was completely identified with centralism and "war economy" methods. Bent on achieving revolutionary shifts in factor allocation and on obtaining the fulfillment of the priority targets as speedily as possible, the Soviet policy makers and planners concentrated their full attention on perfecting the physical balancing of supply and distribution for a number of key products. They discouraged as futile any attempts to combine all these material balances into a single system or to coordinate them fully with all the various balances of value data, such as the balance of income and outlays of the population, the state bank's currency and credit plans, and the government budget. Intent on reaching a number of limited objectives, the planners relied on the rule of providing the top priority branches with ample resources to fulfill and overfulfill their goals, no matter what the impact on other branches. Intuitive selection of goals on the basis of observation of technological trends in the most advanced countries, engineering projection and coordination of the key material balances by successive approximations (successive cuts here and there on either the supply or the allocation side of one balance or another) appeared sufficient to carry the country ahead. No complicated theory was needed for the purpose: model building, the use of abstract formulas and of higher mathematics appeared for many years as impractical to the bureaucrats. The Soviet economic journals turned all their attention to practical, episodic problems.

In the early years of the NEP, the geneticists and most of the economists had stressed that market mechanisms and objectively determined prices were prerequisites of economic calculation and planning. But when Soviet planning actually did start, the officially accepted point of view was that on the contrary prices could not serve for allocative purposes but would be arbitrarily manipulated in order to "raise or lower the capacity of the market within very wide limits." The combined effect of the strategy of forging ahead in the key producer's goods branches, and of the emphasis on the administrative character of Soviet planning ("opposed to automaticity") was to make the bureaucrats visualize agriculture as a sort of bothersome appendix in planning, not as an integral and crucial part of the economy as a whole.

After a number of decades of pragmatic planning, Soviet policy makers, planners, and managers have undoubtedly acquired, through their day-to-day work, an enormous experience in selecting key goals, adjusting physical balances, and carrying out in practice their basic tasks. But this experience is becoming notoriously insufficient today for dealing, in what is now a highly industrialized society, with the increasingly complex problems of setting goals, reaching consistency among them, and achieving efficiency in the use of resources. Fortunately for the Soviet planners, the science of planning has in the meantime made enormous progress in the West. It is from this source that Soviet planners are now borrowing the "abstract models" which Stalin's bureaucracy rejected as cumbersome in the 1920's. The irony of history is that some Western planning tools, such as input-output analysis, are in certain ways related to the pioneering works of Popov, Litoshenko, Barengol'ts, and Fel'dman, but owe nothing at all to the Soviet planning practice of the last thirty years. This practice remains in many respects but a clumsy Sisyphean way of solving the basic problems of a planned economy.

6 Soviet "Corporate" Processes and Problems

As WE have pointed out, the appearance of market imperfections in the mature phase of capitalism, that is, "the monopolization of whole branches of industry," implies for Marxists the cessation within that society of "the absence of a plan."[1] In this theoretical framework the corporate sectors are viewed as islands of purposefully integrated activities emerging within the "chaos" of the market. The socialist state takes over, so to speak, where the monopolies leave off: it organizes the economy as a whole as a single enterprise directed "according to a plan established in advance."[2]

From the beginning of their revolution, the Communists' approach to the problems of management and allocation of resources was based on the ideas of eliminating competition among enterprises, transforming nationalized "factories, workshops, mines and other productive institutions . . . into . . . subdivisions, as it were, of one vast people's workshop, which will embrace the entire national economy," and directing this single corporate aggregate by means of a plan.[3] The debates of the 1920's concerned not the principle of merging all industry and banking into a single national corporate aggregate, managed by the Soviet government, which would allocate all resources, but the ways in which this huge aggregate could be run in practice, the goals which could be set for it and which it could attain, and where and how planning without markets could start.

The origins of the Western type of planning were very different. In the early 1950's Gunnar Myrdal pointed out that the Communists could rightly claim that their planning was not analogous to the "economic planning . . . gradually becoming the recognized frame of economic policies in Western democratic, industrialized countries."[4] In the West, remarked Myrdal, the state has come to assume an increasingly directive role in the economy whenever the growth of corporations and unions has prevented the achievement of automatic equilibrium through atomistic adjustment—that is, when the functioning of the price mechanism is imperiled and when negotiations must be carried out and compromises must be achieved between "the nation-wide interest organizations in the corporate sectors of society."[5] Myrdal added that Western national planning has been further stimulated by the dangers of stagnation and unemployment, the drive toward greater equality of incomes, the expanding size and scope of public finance, and the ensuing deep disturbance of international economic ties.[6]

Since Myrdal wrote, Western attitudes and public policies have continued to evolve but in new directions. Economists and policy makers now stress that economic growth is a public concern and that the government must take deliberate steps to alter the national rate of growth. A large body of opinion still claims that in a free economy the right rate "is that which conforms to the voluntary choices of the people." But an increasing number of economists and policy makers point out that the government is actually faced with an inescapable choice among policy instruments—fiscal and monetary—which have a direct bearing on the level of employment and on the rate of growth. Individual choices necessarily blend with deliberate governmental choices.[7]

Whatever the shifts in Western attitudes, and whatever the apparent similarity in the pursuit of high growth rates both in the East and in the West, Soviet planning can be best understood not in relation to Western governmental planning but in relation to Western corporate processes and problems. Having implanted deliberately, within their backward and illiterate surroundings, the hulk of a giant corporate aggregate, the Russians have tried to work out within this specific framework their own solutions for the management, allocation, and use of resources.

Obviously, while the Western corporation is always immersed in a competitive environment, the single, comprehensive Soviet industrial-banking corporate complex faces no comparable competitor. From its inception, the "competition" of the Soviet corporate aggregate consisted only of "bearing down" on marginal private firms and handicrafts, while its "monopolistic prices" were designed to affect primarily the peasantry.[8] Above all, a competitive environment sets limits beyond which monopolies or oligopolies cannot distort their specific cost-price relationships. No readily apparent standards of orientation are available for a single, all-embracing aggregate whose physical output is arbitrarily divided between investment and consumption. The Soviet corporate complex always absorbs the available investment goods; the costs, profits, and investment of each unit are hardly if at all related; for consumers' goods, what really

matters is that their total value be roughly equal to the wages
paid out by the whole aggregate. In the Western corporation,
objectives of expansion, diversification of products, and
profits may present either an accidental and overlapping accumulation of targets formulated at various functional levels
or a fully integrated program for the organization as a whole.
In the Soviet analogue, economic targets must be fused into
a single program built around some key economic targets,
and these targets must be formulated after taking into account social, political, and military goals; in such a program
profits play only a subordinate role.

Similarities between Soviet and capitalist corporate problems are, on the other hand, striking. From the beginning of
its "all-round" planning era in 1929, the Soviet top leadership
set "intuitively," on the basis of a broad strategy emphasizing the preferential development of certain branches, the
goals of some leading industries, and decided on the capital
expansion needed for fulfilling them. Within this context the
head of each unit, department, and division formulated his
own plan proposals. The top management made the final
decisions and integrations. In fact, even in the largest corporations, the final choice on alternative ways of using corporate resources always rests ultimately with only a few
top line managers;[9] but in the Soviet analogue concentration
of power reached an even higher degree, since both economic and political powers were fused.

Any corporate plan can be both an audacious instrument
of technological change and a shield for conservatism. The
planners can in effect schedule the development of whole
new industrial branches which perhaps might not have developed under normal (market) conditions. On the other

hand, any plan can easily become a haven for inefficiency. Since plans are expressions of intent as well as measures of performance, the operational manager who realizes that he is judged on whether he does or does not attain the objective set in his plan "may set the lowest goals acceptable to his superior." In the Soviet analogue, as in any corporation, "the divisional manager cannot embrace the corporate view, nor can the corporation fully appreciate the pressing problems of operating units."[10] The drive for progress and change from the top is often met by resistance to change at the bottom of the production pyramid.

Corporate planning is necessarily flexible in terms of both tasks and time. Incomplete information, the impossibility of correlating data at all points in time as the plan unfolds, the mixture of managerial intentions, value judgments, intuitions, and objective data, still make planning a managerial process rather than a "system-engineering" or a science.[11] In this, again, Soviet planning can hardly be distinguished from what takes place in most Western corporate aggregates. Flexibility in respect to tasks and time have become characteristic of the Soviet plan; as in any corporate plan, top priorities have always had to be fulfilled no matter what the consequences for other priorities down the line. On the other hand, in any plan, if the present labors necessarily under the shadow of past commitments,[12] the future always seems open to the wildest dreams.

The debates of the 1920's have underlined that in a backward and isolated country the relations between industry and agriculture—in terms of saving, investment, employment, output, etc.—are the crucial ones in the formulation of any over-all economic strategy or of any development plan. The less developed an economy, the more important its agricultural sector, and the more evidently a centralized decision on pattern, pace, and technological options in industrialization —and its attendant decision on the level of investment—becomes essentially a decision on consumption levels and on growth in agriculture itself. The more developed an economy, the less significant usually is agriculture's share in its economic activity as a whole, and the more significant inter-industry relationships become. This may in part explain why detailed input-output tabulations à la Popov, Litoshenko, and Barengol'ts failed to arouse the interest of the Soviet policy makers, for whom the center of the stage was occupied in the initial phase by the relationships between industry and peasant agriculture.

The debates of the 1920's, and the actions which followed them, have shown that patterns of industrialization and development may be set and implemented either as a function of some specific problems typical of a given underdeveloped country, or as a function of the evolving changes in the more developed countries. Investment requirements will vary according to the choice of a specific, individualized solution or of a "competitive" solution keyed to the levels reached in other countries. In order to move on autarkic lines at a rapid pace, the Russians have invested systematically, year in and year out, as much as a quarter of their national income (at current prices),[13] the larger share of which has been channeled toward certain branches of heavy industry. Can such an investment policy be considered economically rational?

To answer this question one must first determine what rate of investment is the economically "rational" rate. In a centrally planned economy, the primary decision on the economic structure desired by the policy maker governs numerous other decisions, including those on the size of investment and on the composition and magnitude of foreign trade. In a country with a large agricultural population, a decision in favor of the priority development of peasant agriculture will probably result in a relatively low ratio of investment to consumption (since consumption on the farm can hardly be reduced below a certain level), large participation in foreign trade, and reliance on comparative advantage. Conversely, emphasis on a fully integrated heavy industry program will lead to high investment requirements, and will perhaps tend over time to make for a lower volume of trade than would be the case with a strategy oriented to comparative advantage (if we can assume that either policy would achieve the same amount of growth in real economic activity). Finally, choices of the pace of development, and of technology—or the intensity of industrialization—will further condition the size of investment needs.

The case for massive investments in the initial phases of industrialization and for the adoption of advanced technology is now well known: only through a major investment effort can one benefit from large-scale techniques and increasing returns; costly though certain modern techniques may appear for countries with redundant labor, they may, in certain branches, make for faster production, tie up less material, and prove cheaper than more primitive techniques. But as Soviet industrialization has shown, the stronger the emphasis on the rapid and intensive development of certain branches with the highest available technology, the sharper will be the ensuing differences between their rate of growth and that of all other branches, and the longer will the most backward methods be retained in the low priority sectors. Thus the triple decision on pattern, pace, and technology determines the over-all target for capital accumulation as well as the more rapid development of industry than of agriculture, the differential growth rates of industrial branches, and the mixture, in various strengths, of capital-intensive and labor-intensive processes throughout the economy as a whole.

The debates of the 1920's drew attention to the need of exploring, for the sake of optimality and efficiency, the connections between the growth rates of industry and agriculture, or as Fel'dman put it, of producers' goods and consumers' goods. But the suggestions of Fel'dman, Kondrat'ev, and Bazarov were set aside. Planning was conducted essentially as an administrative-engineering operation, or as a sum of orders and engineering constructs. Such methods make it possible to focus on a limited number of key projects and goals which are considered as crucial by the policy makers, and to view development as a whole as a function of these key branches only. A poorly responsive price mechanism— and this is the usual case in backward economies—may make physical-engineering planning a necessity if not a virtue, while on the other hand lack of proper information may render optimality and efficiency highly elusive goals. The Soviet bureaucracy was very complacent about this type of "short-cut" to achieve its immediate aims; but the result was that any real progress in planning methods has been achieved not in the country of all-round planning but in the West.

Progress in planning has been further hampered by a number of disparate and debatable solutions sanctioned in Soviet planning theory and practice since the 1920's. The search for consistency and efficiency was discouraged, if not precluded, by emphasis on a so-called "planning principle" supposed to be the "regulator" of a planned economy. This principle simply sanctioned the freedom of the planner to ignore the "law of value" (cost plus price considerations) and led him to distort for either serious or trivial causes both producers' and consumers' prices, and to disregard any market signal. The planners' relative freedom of choice in respect to long-run matters of structure, target setting, and investment priorities (as emphasized by the so-called "teleological" principle) was presumed to hold equally for price setting (as expressed by the so-called "planning" principle). This in turn confused planning with the day-to-day aspects of its implementation, and erased the dividing line between the executive task of the policy maker and planner and the operative functions of the plant manager. Confusion in prices was aggravated rather than corrected when the economy started to move under Stalin along the path of rapid growth: the attachment of the Soviet planners to an organically defective tool for price setting—the labor theory of value—rendered the confusion intolerable when the Soviet Union finally reached a high level of industrialization.

The Soviet model of industrialization—that is, both Soviet strategy and planning procedure—exercises today a deep influence on the underdeveloped areas. The crucial importance within these countries of the relationship between a small industrial and an overwhelming agricultural sector; the decisive importance of massive investments for developing certain new domestic industries, and the possible advantages accruing from the adoption of the advanced technology in at least some key branches and processes; the possibility of automatically fulfilling "realistic" capital formation targets by planning in physical terms, in countries with defective statistical information and unresponsive price mechanisms —all these render the Soviet planning model as it emerged in the 1920's extremely adaptable to backward countries. The antipathy to private enterprise, often identified with colonialism; the currently wide acceptance of the idea that the government necessarily assumes an important role in the consumption, allocation, and management of the country's resources; and finally, the almost charismatic character of the newly independent states[14] render the early Soviet-type planning theory and methods attractive for even non-Communist underdeveloped countries.

If the goal of "reaching and surpassing the highest indices of capitalism" and the strategy of industrialization as formulated in the 1920's remain the unchanged guidelines of Soviet economic policy, still the Soviet policy makers have become aware of the new and more complex organizational and planning problems arising with the increased industrialization of their country. While maintaining the strategy, they have been forced to revise their earlier ideas concerning the operation of the Soviet economy, the role of economic "laws," the alleged antithesis between planning and market relations, and the significance of the price mechanism, to mention but a few things. Increasing awareness of the significance of accurate pricing for complex economic calculation, improvement of the flow of information (mostly in industry), wider use of incentives and of market mechanisms among the "subdivisions" of the Soviet corporate aggregate, reliance on various types of decentralization in respect to some operating managerial tasks, interest in and availability of new programming tools—input-output, linear programming, operations research—render changes in Soviet planning theory and practice both feasible and probable.[15] The Russians stress that theirs is a "commodity-monetary" economy just like that of the capitalist system; that the "law of value" necessarily plays a crucial role; that physical planning must be seriously checked against a variety of value indices. Optimality and economic efficiency are clearly called into play. Obviously, the same strategy can be combined with a number of planning procedures. But although Soviet policy makers have become conscious of this fact and are departing from some of the planning theories and methods of the 1920's —in some respects timorously, in other respects audaciously —other Communist leaders, those of backward China for instance, continue to stick to the old methods of planning, apparently both by conviction and for convenience. Perhaps the crude methods of the 1920's are after all better suited to a lower level of development.

Notes

1. GOALS AND INSTRUMENTS OF ECONOMIC DEVELOPMENT

1. The speed of this race is further accelerated as the policy makers of the more developed countries deliberately aim at quickening the pace of growth of their economies. See E. S. Phelps, ed., *The Goal of Economic Growth* (New York: Norton, 1962), pp. vii ff.

2. See *Vsesoiuznaia Kommunisticheskaia Partiia (Bol'shevikov) v rezoliutsiiakh i resheniiakh S'ezdov, Konferentsii i Plenumov Tsk* (All-Union Communist Party [Bolsheviks], resolutions and decisions of Congresses, Conferences and Plenums of the Central Committee), Sixth Edition (Moscow: Gospolitizdat, 1941), Part I (1898-1924), p. 545.

3. Ibid., Part II (1925-1939), p. 49. The XIVth Party Conference had affirmed in April of the same year that the triumph of socialism was possible in one country, but had added the qualification that a "final guarantee" against capitalist restoration depended "on the victory of socialism in some advanced countries at least" (p. 28).

4. Marxian economics is a *"Stufenlehre"*: its objective, as P. J. D. Wiles rightly points out, is to discover through what institutional stages (*Stufen*) the world economy is passing and to *make* "things go in the direction desired or predicted." See P. J. D. Wiles, *The Political Economy of Communism* (Cambridge: Harvard University Press, 1963), pp. 47-48.

5. *Vsesoiuznaia Kommunisticheskaia Partiia . . . resoliutsiiakh* (All-Union Communist Party . . . resolutions), Part II, p. 125.

6. The 1928 Soviet income was estimated by Julius Wyler at $20.2 billion in 1940 dollar prices. We have converted the Wyler data to

131

1954 prices. See J. Wyler, "The National Income of Soviet Russia," *Social Research*, December 1946; and "Die Schätzungen des sowjet-russichen Volkseinkommens," *Schweizerische Zeitschrift für Volkswirtschaft und Statistik* (1951), nos. 5 and 6.

7. The Soviet population reached 150.4 million in the mid-twenties; that of Brazil reached 58.4 million in the mid-fifties. The territories of the two countries covered 21.0 and 8.0 million sq. km.

8. Quoted by Leon Trotsky, *The Real Situation in Russia*, trans. by Max Eastman (New York: Harcourt, Brace, 1928), p. 23.

2. THE SOVIET ECONOMY AND ECONOMIC LAWS

1. Karl Marx, *A Contribution to the Critique of Political Economy*, trans. by N. I. Stone (Chicago: Kerr and Co., 1911), p. 11.

2. Ibid., pp. 11-12.

3. Paraphrasing Marshall, we could say that for Marx economic "laws" are exact statements of economic tendencies; Marshall's, and modern, principles are only statements of probable tendencies. See Alfred Marshall, *Principles of Economics* (London: Macmillan, 1961), vol. 1, pp. 31 ff.

4. See A. Bogdanov, *A Short Course of Economic Science*, Second Edition (London: Dorrit Press, 1927), p. 14. Also G. V. Plekhanov, *The Materialist Conception of History* (London: Lawrence and Wishart, 1940), p. 28; and Marx, *A Contribution to the Critique of Political Economy*, pp. 265, 268-269, 272.

5. The recognition of the existence of a "law" (or an objective regularity), and conformity with it, is called in Russian *zakonomernost'*. "Determinism" is only a very approximate translation of the term.

6. Marx's economic analysis leaves no room for subjective concepts concerning cost, price, or demand. For Marx, individual households or entrepreneurs can never be viewed as isolated atoms or as Robinson Crusoes, but only as parts of a given social system. Values and demand-supply relationships are determined by the mode of production and social labor relationships—or by the "productive relations" which this mode of production conditions. Modern value theory (or, in Soviet parlance, "bourgeois" economics) embraces two distinct types of analysis. The first deals with the individual behavior of entrepreneurs or households in terms of their own motivations; the second ascertains how interaction of these individual entities determines, independently

of rational will, their demand-supply relationships. Cf. N. I. Bukharin, *Ekonomika perekhodnogo perioda* (Economics of the period of transition) (Moscow: Gosizdat, 1920), p. 126; and W. Leontief, "The Significance of Marxian Economics for Present Day Economic Theory," *American Economic Review*, Supplement, XXVIII (1938), 1: 1-2. The Marxists view Marxian economics as resting on "objectivist-social" foundations, while "bourgeois" economics rests on subjectivist foundations.

This crucial difference between Marxist and non-Marxist approaches to economics should not be confused with the voluntarist-subjectivist versus determinist-objectivist argument concerning the importance and the limits of the "conscious" element in shaping up a socialist society. Under socialism man is thought to "more and more consciously make his own history," since the "social causes set in motion by him will have in the main and in a constantly growing measure, the results intended by him." F. Engels, "Socialism: Utopian and Scientific," in A. P. Mendel, ed., *Essential Works of Marxism* (New York: Bantam, 1961), p. 80. The Soviet determinists emphasized in this connection the role of the economic milieu in which the party necessarily exercises its actions.

7. N. I. Bukharin and E. A. Preobrazhenskii, *The ABC of Communism*, trans. by Eden and Cedar Paul for the Communist Party of Great Britain (London: Unwin Bros., 1922).

8. Ibid., pp. 334-335. Presumably the authors refer specifically to money prices and not to planners' use of ratios of equivalence between products for accounting purposes.

9. See N. I. Bukharin, *Ekonomika perekhodnogo perioda* (Economics of the period of transition), p. 125.

10. Ibid., p. 129. See also Paul M. Sweezy, *The Theory of Capitalist Development: Principles of Marxian Political Economy* (New York: Oxford University Press, 1942), pp. 52-53.

11. See I. Stepanov-Skvortsov, "Chto takoe politicheskaia ekonomiia?" (What is political economy?) and "Preniia po dokladu I. Stepanova-Skvortsova" (Discussion on the report of I. Stepanov-Skvortsov), *Vestnik kommunisticheskoi akademii* (Moscow: Komakadizdat, no. 11, 1925), p. 269.

Before the debate in the Communist Academy the economist V. G. Groman published, in connection with the discussion on planning, an article entitled "O nekotorykh zakonomernostiakh empiricheski obnaruzhivaemykh v nashem narodnom khoziaistve" (On certain regularities empirically observable in our economy), *Planovoe khoziaistvo* (1925),

1: 88-101. Groman stressed the existence of "a system of empirical laws" operating within the Soviet economy, and he affirmed his desire to uncover the prevailing "economic static and dynamic regularities." As we shall see in the discussion on planning, Groman's position was severely attacked by those who stressed the importance of "conscious" factors in planning.

12. Stepanov-Svortsov, "Chto takoe politicheskaia ekonomiia?" (What is political economy?), p. 287.

13. Ibid., p. 302.

14. Ibid., pp. 296, 298, 315.

15. Ibid., p. 310.

16. See B. Borilin, "Lenin ob 'Ekonomike perekhodnogo perioda'" (Lenin on the "Economics of the transition period"), *Bol'shevik* (October 1929), no. 20. Quoting Lenin's marginal notes on Bukharin's work—made nine years earlier—Borilin adds: "The limitation of political economy to the frame of commodity-capitalism which is given by com. Bukharin [and *still* by the majority of Marxists in the USSR] is, according to Lenin, erroneous and represents a step back on Engel's opinion. Lenin believes that political economy must exist also under communism" (p. 30; emphasis supplied).

17. J. V. Stalin, *Economic Problems of Socialism in the USSR* (New York: International Publishers, 1952), p. 19. (Emphasis supplied.)

18. Ibid.

19. Ibid.

20. It is interesting to note that in vol. 51 (1945) of the *Bol'shaia sovetskaia entsiklopediia* (The great Soviet encyclopedia), First Edition, one reads under the entry "Skvortsov-Stepanov" that Skvortsov-Stepanov, though a good Bolshevik, was influenced by Bogdanov and displayed a "mechanist understanding of Marxism" (p. 283). The Second Edition of *Bol'shaia*, released in 1955, drops any reference to Skvortsov-Stepanov's "mechanist understanding of Marxism."

21. O. Lange, *The Political Economy of Socialism*, lecture on November 18, 1957 at the Institute of International Politics and Economics, in Belgrade (Warsaw: Polish Institute of International Affairs, 1957), pp. 5-8. (Mimeographed.)

22. Ibid., p. 5.

23. See K. N. Shafiev, et al., eds., *Politicheskaia ekonomiia sotsializma* (Political economy of socialism) (Moscow: Sotsekgiz, 1960), pp. 179-180, 184.

24. Ibid., p. 118.

25. See N. Spulber, *The Soviet Economy: Structure, Principles, Problems* (New York: Norton, 1962), ch. 9.

26. For a discussion of this point see Wiles, *The Political Economy of Communism*, pp. 55-56.

27. See K. Marx, *Capital*, II (Moscow: Foreign Languages Publishing House, 1957), pp. 392 ff.

28. See Spulber, *The Soviet Economy*, pp. 131 ff.

29. G. A. Fel'dman, "K teorii tempov narodnogo dokhoda" (On the theory of growth rates of national income), *Planovoe khoziaistvo* (1928), 11: 146-171, and (1928) 12: 151-181.

30. See Evsey D. Domar, "A Soviet Model of Growth," in *Essays in the Theory of Economic Growth* (New York: Oxford University Press, 1957), pp. 223 ff.

31. Ibid.

32. E. A. Preobrazhenskii, "Khoziaistvennoe ravnovesie v sisteme SSSR" (Economic equilibrium in the Soviet system), *Vestnik Kommunisticheskoi Akademii* (1927), 22: 19-71.

33. See notably R. S. Eckaus, "The Factor Proportions Problem in Underdeveloped Areas," *American Economic Review*, September 1955, pp. 539-565; A. O. Hirschman, "Investment Policies and 'Dualism' in Underdeveloped Countries," *American Economic Review*, September 1957, pp. 550-570; Sayre P. Schatz, "Inflation in Underdeveloped Areas: A Theoretical Analysis," ibid., pp. 571-593.

34. See for instance P. C. Mahalanobis, "Some Observations on the Process of Growth of National Income," *Sankhya*, XII (1953); and "The Approach of Operational Research to Planning in India," *Sankhya*, XVI (1955). For presentation of Professor Mahalanobis' models— a two-sector model (sector one producing investment goods, sector two producing consumers' goods only) and a four-sector model (derived from the former by subdividing consumer goods industries into [a] factory production of consumer goods, [b] consumer goods, including agricultural products, in small and household industries, and [c] services such as health and education)—as well as for analysis of the problems raised by the allocation of investment over these four sectors, see Jan Tinbergen and H. C. Boz, *Mathematical Models of Economic Growth* (New York: McGraw-Hill, 1962), pp. 77-80.

35. P. I. Popov, ed., *Balans narodnogo khoziaistva Soiuza SSR 1923/24 goda* (Balance of the national economy of the USSR for

1923/24), *Trudy Tsentral'nogo Statisticheskogo Upravleniia* (Trans-actions of the Central Statistical Administration), XXIX (Moscow: Central Statistical Administration, 1926).

36. S. G. Strumilin, "O kontrol'nykh tsifrakh Gosplana" (On the control figures of Gosplan), in S. G. Strumilin, ed., *Ocherki sovetskoi ekonomike: Resursy i perspektivy* (Essays in Soviet economics: Re-sources and perspectives) (Moscow-Leningrad: USSR Gosplan, 1928), p. 311.

37. The editorial "Put' Sovetskoi Statistiki" (The road of Soviet statistics), *Vestnik statistiki*, XXV (1927), 1: 15.

38. V. G. Groman, "Balans narodnogo khoziaistva" (Balance of the national economy), *Planovoe khoziaistvo* (1926), 11: 62-80. Dr. Naum Jasny contends that the "idea of the balance of national econ-omy (the USA input-output analysis) was first advanced in the U.S.S.R. (in the twentieth century)" and that this "idea was first brought up by V. G. Groman in early 1923 at the latest." See Naum Jasny, *Essays on the Soviet Economy* (New York: Praeger, 1962), pp. 54, 161-162. Dr. Jasny seems to imply that a balance of the national economy is necessarily identical with input-output analysis and that Groman first advanced this idea. Actually, there were a number of economists both in Russia and abroad who suggested a variety of national balance schemes; but only Popov and Litoshenko constructed a flow table which prefigured an elementary input-output tabulation. And, as we have said, their methodology was rejected by Groman. For a review of some theories concerning a national economic balance see P. Hermberg, *Volkswirtschaftliche Bilanzen* (National Economic Balances) (Leipzig: Akademische Verlagsgesellschaft, 1927), which includes *inter alia* ref-erences to various German works dating into the late nineteenth cen-tury; and S. A. Fal'ker, "Iz istorii idei narodnokhoziaistvennogo bal-ansa" (From the history of the idea of a national economic balance), *Planovoe khoziaistvo* (1928), 10: 153-174. The merit of Popov and Litoshenko is not that they proposed the drawing of a balance, but that they constructed one which revealed all the concurrent input-out-put aspects of the activity of all the branches of the Soviet economy of the time. For this they owe hardly anything to their predecessors, particularly Groman. But of course it is still a long way from Popov's descriptive pioneering attempt to modern input-output analysis, par-ticularly the use of technical coefficients, the ability to express the struc-tural interdependence of any economy, and the capacity to project all interrelations in a consistent way.

39. See W. Leontief, "Balans narodnogo khoziaistva SSSR" (The balance of the national economy of the USSR), *Planovoe khoziaistvo* (1925), 12: 254-258. Professor Leontief dealt in his review with Popov's report to the Council for Labor and Defense, published in *Ekonomicheskaia zhizn'* (1925), no. 72.

40. R. E. Vaisberg, "Burzhuaznaia ideologiia v ekonomicheskoi literature" (Bourgeois ideology in economic literature), *Planovoe khoziaistvo* (1925), no. 11.

41. R. E. Vaisberg in "K postroeniiu general'nogo plana" (On the construction of the General Plan), "Doklad N. A. Kovalevskogo i preniia po dokladu N. A. Kovalevskogo" (Report of N. A. Kovalevskii and discussion on the report), *Planovoe khoziaistvo* (1930), 3: 146.

42. See M. Barengol'ts, "Emkost' promyshlennogo rynka v SSSR" (Capacity of the industrial market in the USSR), *Planovoe khoziaistvo* (1928), 7: 325-348. Nobody then took the next step, namely, that of relating the output of a sector to the demand of other sectors, and of revealing the "interdependence coefficients" of the economy.

43. R. Riabushkin, "Balansovye postroeniia v burzhuaznoi statistike" (Construction of balance sheets in bourgeois statistics), *Vestnik statistiki* (1956), no. 6: 50-59.

44. See Academician V. S. Nemchinov, *Application of Statistical and Mathematical Methods in Soviet Planning*, Report to the International Conference on Input-Output Analysis (Moscow: Academy of Sciences of the USSR, 1961), pp. 16-17.

3. STRATEGIES OF ECONOMIC DEVELOPMENT

1. But opinions at present are increasingly divided as to the need for a government policy expressly designed to alter the rate of growth of the economy as a whole. See E. S. Phelps, ed., *The Goal of Economic Growth* (New York: Norton, 1962).

2. See V. I. Lenin, *The Development of Capitalism in Russia: The Process of the Formation of a Home Market for Large-scale Industry* (1899) (Moscow: Foreign Languages Publishing House, 1956).

3. As Lenin put it, "the home market grows not so much on account of articles of consumption as of means of production." Ibid., p. 31.

4. Ibid., pp. 31-32.

5. The contention that technological progress always implies an increase in the organic composition of capital is questionable. Tech-

nological progress may be achieved in a number of ways, including replacement of worn-out equipment, that is, at a zero rate of growth of sector I. For further comments see N. Spulber, *The Soviet Economy: Structure, Principles, Problems* (New York: Norton, 1962), pp. 211, 212.

6. See Maurice Dobb, *Russian Economic Development Since the Revolution* (New York: Dutton, 1928), p. 245.

7. The so-called Left Opposition (Moscow Opposition, Opposition of 1923, or Trotskyists) solidified in 1923 around Trotsky after a denunciation of his views by the ruling group of the party (Stalin, Zinoviev, and Bukharin) in the beginning of October of that year. In a collective letter addressed to the Central Committee of the party (and known since then as the "Declaration of the 46") forty-six prominent Communists sided with Trotsky on a number of problems ranging from the role of industry to the fight against "bureaucratism." Among the signatories were Piatakov, Preobrazhenskii, Serebriakov, Smirnov, Boguslavskii, Stukhov, Yakovleva, Kossior, Rafael, Maximovskii, Beloborodov, Alskii, Muralov, Rosengol'ts, Sosnovskii, Voronskii, Bosh, Drobnis, and Eltsin. In 1926 the group was joined by the so-called Leningrad Opposition, led by Zinoviev, Kamenev, Sokol'nikov, Krupskaia, Slutskii, and others. The resultant fusion created the Opposition Bloc of Bolshevik-Leninists. See Leon Trotsky, *The Third International After Lenin*, trans. by John Wright (New York: Pioneer Publishers, 1957), pp. 314-315.

8. Cf. *Vsesoiuznaia Kommunisticheskaia Partiia (Bol'shevikov) v rezoliutsiiakh i resheniiakh S'ezdov, Konferentsii i Plenumov Tsk* (All-Union Communist Party [Bolsheviks], resolutions and decisions of Congresses, Conferences and Plenums of the Central Committee), Sixth Edition (Moscow: Gospolitizdat, 1941), Part I, p. 545. The policy was confirmed at the XIIIth Party Congress in May of the same year.

9. The Russians define as "recovery" period the period in which prewar levels of output, particularly in industry and agriculture, have been reached. By "reconstruction" they understand the expansion of productive capacity, a shift of the economy to a "higher technological plane," and a change in pace of capital formation and in rates of growth of the main sectors of the economy.

10. L. Shanin, "Ekonomicheskaia priroda nashego bestovar'ia" (The economic nature of our commodity shortage), *Ekonomicheskoe obozrenie* (1926), 11: 25-39; and "Voprosy ekonomicheskogo kursa" ("Questions of the economic course"), *Bol'shevik* (1926), 2: 65-87.

11. N. I. Bukharin, *Partiia i oppozitsionnyi blok* (The party and the opposition bloc) (Leningrad: Priboi, 1926), p. 41.

12. N. I. Bukharin, *La situation extérieure et intérieure de l'URSS* (The foreign and domestic situation of the USSR), Report to the XVth Party Conference (Paris: Bureau d'Editions, 1927), p. 47. In terms of the current discussions on underdevelopment, Bukharin raises implicitly the question of aggregate demand and that of the linkage between the emergence of new wants and expectations in the rural areas and the expenditure there of additional efforts to increase output. As A. Smithies puts it, "a programme that delays unduly the realization of these expectations may not be the most efficient in achieving the desired increases in output"— i.e., may not stimulate more work if additional goods are not obtainable, and may thus hinder the growth of industry. See A. Smithies, "Rising Expectations and Economic Development," *The Economic Journal*, June 1961, p. 259.

13. Commenting on the decisions of the XVth All-Union Party Conference, the official *History of the Communist Party of the Soviet Union* records that "the Conference noted that the hegemony of large-scale industry in the country's economy had been strengthened, that *its leading role in promoting the development of agriculture,* including agricultural co-operation, had grown." (Emphasis supplied.) Stress continued to be placed on the role of heavy industry as the lever for transforming agriculture. See B. N. Ponomaryov et al., *History of the Communist Party of the Soviet Union* (Moscow: Foreign Languages Publishing House, 1960), p. 410.

14. See E. A. Preobrazhenskii, *Novaia ekonomika* (New economics), Second Edition (Moscow: Komakadizdat, 1926).

15. Some Western writers agree that a major economic change in an underdeveloped country—in Soviet parlance, its shifting to a higher technological plane—does require capital deepening and thus runs counter to "the dictates of the relative factor-supply situation." H. J. Bruton, for instance, notes that "where the capital-labour ratio calls for labour-using, capital-saving innovations, modern technology calls for a series of innovations which are the exact opposite *before* the capital-saving innovations are possible." (See H. J. Bruton, "Growth Models and Underdeveloped Economies," *The Journal of Political Economy*, August, 1955, pp. 327-328.) While, however, Lenin (cf. above, note 5) and Preobrazhenskii assert that technological progress is always capital-using, the modern literature concedes at most that this may be typical for the initial phase during which an attempt is made by an

underdeveloped country to reorganize its general economic system. Capital-using innovations are viewed in the context of the Western thesis as necessary *before* capital-saving innovations become possible.

16. The empilical assumptions implicit in Preobrazhenskii's argument are questionable: it is not always true that small-scale production has a higher ratio of fixed capital to output than does large-scale, or a higher ratio of inventory to output. Currently the more usual assumptions—likewise empirically precarious—are the opposite.

17. R. S. Eckaus demonstrates in his analysis of factor proportions applied to two sectors that "disguised unemployment in the rural sector will increase if a large part of the capital available is systematically drawn into the capital-intensive and fixed-coefficient sector." See "The Factor Proportions Problem in Underdeveloped Areas," *American Economic Review*, September 1955, pp. 559-560.

18. See L. Trotsky, "Platform of the Opposition" (1927), published in English under the title *The Real Situation in Russia*, trans. by Max Eastman. (New York: Harcourt, Brace, 1928), pp. 63, 67.

19. See "Perspektivy khoziaistvennogo razvitiia SSSR: Kontrol'nye tsifry Gosplana" (Perspectives of the economic development of the USSR: Control figures of the State Planning Committee), Report of V. P. Miliutin at the Communist Academy, and Piatakov's comments, *Vestnik kommunisticheskoi akademii* (1926), 17: 208 ff.

20. The level of savings is far from being the only growth-inhibiting factor. Many other growth-inhibiting elements—shortages of specific commodities, skills, organization, and foreign exchange—weigh heavily on the capacity for development of certain underdeveloped areas. Various modern writers therefore suggest that a narrow-minded preoccupation with the supply of savings leads only to a single-tracked emphasis on consumer austerity, while a strategy concerned with coping with specific scarcities offers better avenues for attacking the various dimensions of the problem of development. See John P. Lewis, *Quiet Crisis in India: Economic Development and American Policy* (Washington: Brookings Institution, 1962), pp. 35 ff.

21. See J. V. Stalin, "Industrialization and the Right Deviation in the C.P.S.U. (b)" (1928), *Works*, XI (Moscow: Foreign Languages Publishing House, 1954), p. 256.

22. See Z. S. Katsenelenbaum, *Industrializatsiia khoziaistva i zadachi kredita v SSSR* (Industrialization of the economy and the tasks of credit in the USSR) (Moscow-Leningrad: Gosizdat, 1928).

23. See the key document of the party's XVth Congress, "O direktivakh po sostavleniiu piatiletnego plana narodnogo khoziaistva" (Di-

rectives on the drawing of the Five-Year Plan of the national economy)
(December 1927), in *Vsesoiuznaia Kommunisticheskaia Partiia . . .
rezoliutsiiakh* (All-Union Communist Party . . . resolutions), Part II,
pp. 237 ff.

24. See Spulber, *The Soviet Economy*, pp. 36-37, 230.

25. See Gosplan SSSR, Kontrol'nye tsifry narodnogo khoziaistva na
1926/27 god (Control figures of the national economy for 1926/27)
(Moscow: *Planovoe khoziaistvo*, 1926), pp. 170-171. The idea of the
joint development of industry and agriculture at a differential pace,
"on the U.S. model," stressed by the party's XVth Congress, was
widely popularized at the time. See V. E. Motylev, *Problema tempa
razvitiia SSSR* (The problem of the pace of development of the USSR)
(Moscow: Komakadizdat, 1928), p. 103.

26. V. A. Bazarov, "Printsipy postroeniia perspektivnogo plana"
(Principles of long-range planning), *Planovoe khoziaistvo* (1928), 2:
38-63.

27. See below, chapter five, "Principles and Procedures of Planning."

28. For a number of reasons which I have summarized elsewhere,
Communist China has followed since the mid-1950's Bukharin's rather
than Preobrazhenskii's approach. See my paper on "Contrasting Economic Patterns: Chinese and Soviet Development Strategies," *Soviet
Studies*, July 1963.

For the discussions on "balanced" versus "unbalanced" growth in the
current literature on development see notably A. O. Hirschman, *The
Strategy of Economic Development* (New Haven: Yale University
Press, 1958), chs. 3 and 4, and P. Streeten, *Economic Integration: Aspects and Problems* (Leyden: Sythoff, 1961) ch. V.

29. The whole belt-tightening strategy of the Left obviously depended upon the political and social feasibility of "declaring war on the
peasants" and of maintaining a regimen of rigorous authoritarian controls. Evidently this cannot be accomplished in a country committed
to democratic processes. On the other hand, even in a Communist dictatorship the share of produce extracted from a very backward agriculture might not be sufficient to sustain a vast program of industrialization and urbanization. Unable sufficiently to expand the marketed
share of grains, the Chinese adopted a different strategy: they organ-
ized a massive mobilization of rural manpower for capital construction both inside and outside agriculture. See my "Contrasting Economic
Patterns: Chinese and Soviet Development Strategies," *Soviet Studies*,
July 1963.

30. See G. M. Krzhizhanovskii, "Oblastnye elektricheskie stantsii na

torfe i ikh znachenie dlia tsentral'nogo promyshlennogo raiona Rossii" (Regional electric stations using peat and their importance for the central industrial region of Russia). This article, written in November 1915, is included in *Izbranoe* (Selected works) (Moscow: Gospolitizdat, 1957), pp. 9-20. See also pp. 50, 56.

31. See G. M. Krzhizhanovskii, "Piat' let bor'by za plan" (Five years of struggle for the plan), *Planovoe khoziaistvo* (1926), 3: 13.

32. See G. M. Krzhizhanovskii's article, "Plan elektrifikatsii RSFSR" (The Plan of electrification of Russia), written in December 1920 and reprinted in *Izbranoe* (Selected works), pp. 65-189. Marvelous prospects were foreseen in the twenties from the massive use of electricity. Bazarov, for instance, declared that thanks to its fractionability and transportability, electricity would allow both the mechanization of handicrafts and the reduction of urban construction, a fact which would "relegate to the museums of the future socialist society . . . the barrack-type factory and their fitting social complement the skyscraper buildings . . . the most glaring manifestation of the cultural barbarity produced by the crude technology of the age of classical capitalism." See also V. Bazarov, "Printsipy postoeniia perspektivnogo plana" (Principles of long-range planning), *Planovoe khoziaistvo* (1928), 2: 38-63. A young technician, I. Ivanov, stressed in a famous article highly praised by Krzhizhanovskii that electricity would serve as the basis for Communist technology in the same way that steam power had served as the foundation of early capitalist technology. The Communist virtues of electricity were supposed to stem from the fact that electricity "could be dispensed from a single automated central station, through a single mechanism, to a scattered system of working machines." (See I. Ivanov, "Materialnyi bazis kommunisticheskogo obshchestva" (The material basis of communist society), *Vestnik sotsialisticheskoi akademii*, IV (1923), 169-185.

33. The plan was drawn by a State Commission for the Electrification of Russia (Gosudarstvennaia Komissiia po Elektrifikatsii Rossii, abbreviated as GOELRO).

4. EFFICIENCY AND THE RATE OF GROWTH

1. Cf. Resolution of the XIVth Party Congress, in *Vesoiuznaia Kommunisticheskaia Partiia (Bol'shevikov) v rezoliutsiiakh i resheniiakh S'ezdov, Konferentsii i Plenumov Tsk* (All-Union Communist Party

[Bol'sheviks], resolutions and decisions of Congresses, Conferences and Plenums of the Central Committee), Sixth Edition (Moscow: Gospolitizdat, 1941), Part II, pp. 49-50.

2. Ibid., p. 125.

3. V. A. Bazarov, "O metodologii postroeniia perspektivnykh planov" (On the methodology for drafting perspective plans), *Planovoe khoziaistvo* (1926), 7: 7-21.

4. See V. A. Bazarov, "O 'vostanovitel'nykh protsessakh' voobshche i ob 'emissionnykh vozmozhnostiakh' v chastnosti" (On the recovery process" in general and on the "possibilities of currency emission" in particular), *Ekonomicheskoe obozrenie* (1925), 1: 11-29.

Colin Clark—a kind of latter-day Bazarovist—affirms that such a theory should be "a commonplace of economics though many prominent economists have in fact failed to see it." "When a country is recovering from wars, invasions, and similar disasters," adds Clark, "there will be a recovery period in which growth is rapid, followed by a period of gradually decelerating growth as productivity approaches that position on its normal trend which it might have been expected to reach had the war not occurred." See C. Clark, *The Real Productivity of Soviet Russia: A Critical Evaluation,* Committee on the Judiciary, 87th Congress (Washington: Government Printing Office, 1961), p. 2.

5. See V. E. Motylev, *Problema tempa razvitiia SSSR* (The problem of the pace of development of the USSR) (Moscow: Komakadizdat, 1928), p. 116.

6. G. M. Krzhizhanovskii, ed., *Kontrol'nye tsifry narodnogo khoziaistva na 1928/29 god* (Control figures of the national economy for 1928/29) (Moscow: USSR Gosplan, 1929), Introduction, pp. 11-19.

7. See A. Boiarskii, "O teorii zatukhaiushchego tempa razvitiia sovetskogo khoziaistva" (On the theory of decelerating growth rates of the Soviet economy), *Planovoe khoziaistvo* (1930), 10-11: 158 ff.

8. G. A. Fel'dman, "O limitakh industrializatsii" (On the limits of industrialization), *Planovoe khoziaistvo* (1929), 2: 184 ff. It is interesting to note that in all his other papers Fel'dman points to the *upper* limits of industrialization, namely, the capacity of his sector u, the rate of growth in the efficiency of its utilization, its expansion, and its relation to the total capital of sector p. See above, pp. 40-42.

9. Zolotarev's paper, published in *Torgovo-promyshlennaia gazeta* (December 7, 1929), is criticized by E. I. Kviring in "Problemy general'nogo plana" (Problems of the General Plan), *Planovoe khoziaistvo* (1930), 4: 5 ff.

10. See L. M. Sabsovich, "Gipoteza mashtabov produktsii osnovykh otraslei narodnogo khoziaistva SSSR v period general'nogo plana" (Hypothesis concerning the production scale of main branches of the USSR's economy during the period of the General Plan), *Planovoe khoziaistvo* (1929), 1: 64. An expanded but simplified version of the same paper, prepared for mass distribution, was *SSSR cherez 10 let* (USSR in 10 years) (Moscow: Moskovskii Rabochii, 1930).

11. N. Kovalevskii, "K postroeniiu general'nogo plana" (On the construction of the General Plan), *Planovoe khoziaistvo* (1930), 3: 140.

12. Soviet planning continues to proceed from *micro*-economic de- cisions (output targets for given industries) to *macro*-economic calcu- lations (the volume and the rate of growth of national income, and its distribution). The basic decisions concern, as we have already pointed out, intermediate (so-called producers') goods. See also below, ch. 5.

13. See Motylev, *Problema tempa razvitiia SSSR* (The problem of the pace of development of the USSR), pp. 107, 111, 125, 129. See also E. Zaleski, *Planification de la croissance et fluctuations économ- iques en URSS*) (Planning of growth and economic fluctuations in the USSR), vol. I (1918-32) (Paris: Sedes, 1962), pp. 71 ff.

14. On the shortcomings of Soviet statistical computations and on the distorted nature of the 1926/27 weights see Spulber, *The Soviet Economy*, pp. 142 ff.

15. L. Trotsky, *Soviet Economy in Danger* (New York: Pioneer Publishers, 1932), pp. 35 ff.

16. This point is interestingly elaborated for Communist China's early economic planning by Yuan-li Wu, in association with Robert J. Barr and K. N. Chiang, in a draft report circulated by the authors, *Potentialities and Projections of the Chinese Economy, 1958 and Be- yond* (mimeographed).

17. See Maurice Dobb, *An Essay on Economic Growth and Plan- ning* (London: Routledge and Kegan Paul, 1960), pp. 66-75.

18. The repression against "bourgeois spets" (specialists)—engineers, managers, economists, planners—started in May 1928 with the trial of the engineers of Donbas. It reached its climax in 1930 during the trials of the Moscow industrial executives and of the Mensheviks. Two thousand persons were involved for alleged "sabotage" and complicity to "sabotage" in the trial of the industrial executives: prominent among the accused was I. Kalinnikov, a pioneer of Soviet long-term planning

and a member of the presidium of Gosplan. The trial ended with five death sentences, later changed to prison terms. See *Le Procès des industriels de Moscou*, 25 novembre-8 décembre 1930, sténographie intégrale des débats (The trial of the Moscow industrial executives, November 25-December 8, 1930, stenographic report) (Paris: Valois, 1931). For the early role of Kalinnikov see S. G. Strumilin, "Pervye opyty perspektivnogo planirovaniia" (First experiences with perspective planning), *Planovoe khoziaistvo* (1930), 12: 299 ff., reprinted in S. G. Strumilin, *Na planovom fronte* (On the planning front) (Moscow: Gospolitizdat, 1958), pp. 274 ff.

The second big trial of 1930 indicted the Bureau of the so-called "Counter-Revolutionary Menshevik Organization." The indictment alleged that the Mensheviks aimed at "the disorganization of the national economic life of the country, the destruction and undermining of socialist construction and particularly the *retardation of the tempo* of reconstruction." In the twisted way typical of the Stalinist trials of the 1930's, the former Menshevik Ginzburg was forced to state that his "two methods of sabotage" were the concomitant planning of "an exaggerated over-strained tempo of development or a reduced and very limited tempo." See *The Menshevik Trial, Text of the Indictment of the Counter-Revolutionary Menshevik Organization* (New York: Workers Library Publishers, 1931?) pp. 11, 57, 58.

19. Cf. Resolution of the XIVth Party Congress, in *Vsesoiuznaia Kommunisticheskaia Partiia . . . rezoliutsiiakh* (All-Union Communist Party . . . resolutions), Part II, p. 238.

20. See above, pp. 43, 82-83.

21. Discussion on N. A. Kovalevskii, "K postroeniiu general'nogo plana" (On the construction of the General Plan), *Planovoe khoziaistvo* (1930), 3: 146.

22. Ibid., p. 149.

23. Ibid., pp. 155-156.

24. N. N. Shaposhnikov, "Ob osnovnykh printsipakh industrializatsii" (On the fundamental principles of industrialization), *Ekonomicheskoe obozrenie* (1929), 1: 42 ff.

25. R. Gol'dberg, "O metodakh ischisleniia effektivnosti kapital'nykh vlozhenii" (Methods of calculating the efficiency of capital investments), *Puti industrializatsii* (1929), 11: 10 ff.

26. S. Rozentul, "Formula effektivnosti kapital'nykh vlozhenii" (Formula of efficiency of capital investments), *Planovoe khoziaistvo* (1929), 6: 99-116.

27. See L. Iushkov, "Osnovnoi vopros planovoi metodologii: Metody planirovaniia kapital'nykh zatrat po linii maksimal'noi ikh effektivnosti" (The basic problem of planning methodology: The method of planning capital investment and of maximizing its effectiveness), *Vestnik finansov* (1928), 10: 26 ff.

28. Ia. Rozenfel'd, "Problema ischisleniia effektivnosti kapital'nykh vlozhenii v sovetskoi promyshlenosti" (Problem of calculating the effectiveness of capital investments in Soviet industry), *Puti industrializatsii* (1929), 20: 24 ff.

29. See G. Abezgauz, "Effektivnost' vlozheniia kapitalov v sovetskom khoziaistve i metody ee ischisleniia" (Effectiveness of capital investment in the Soviet economy and methods of its calculation), *Puti industrializatsii* (1928), 18: 24 ff.

30. M. Barun, "Ob effektivnosti kapital'nogo stroitel'stva promyshlenosti" (On effectiveness of capital construction in industry), *Puti industrializatsii* (1928), 3: 12-26.

31. L. Litoshenko, "Problema effektivnosti kapital'nykh vlozhenii" (The problem of effectiveness of capital investment), *Vestnik finansov* (1928), 1; 40-57 and 3: 20-40.

32. Krzhizhanovskii, ed., Kontrol'nye tsifry narodnogo khoziaistva *na 1928/29 god* (Control figures of the national economy for 1928/29), Introduction.

33. It is interesting to compare the following declaration of N. S. Khrushchev, made in 1959, with Sabsovich's predictions made thirty years earlier: "To surpass the level in the United States means to exceed the highest indexes of capitalism. The fact that we are now setting ourselves this task shows how much our forces, our possibilities have grown. . . . Based on the pace of industrial development in the USSR and the United States, the Soviet Union will, as a result of the fulfillment of the [Seven-Year] Plan with regard to absolute output of certain most important kinds of production, surpass, and with regard to others approach, the present level of industrial production in the United States. By that time the output of most important agricultural produce both in absolute figures and in per capita production will surpass the present output in the United States. . . . Therefore, if we calculate on a per capita basis, we shall probably need, after the fulfillment of the Seven-Year Plan, about five more years to catch up with and outstrip the United States in industrial output. Thus, by that time, or perhaps even sooner, the Soviet Union will advance to first place in the world

both in absolute volume of production and in per capita production."
Declaration of N. S. Khrushchev, XXth Party Congress, *Pravda*, January 28, 1959.

5. PRINCIPLES AND PROCEDURES OF PLANNING

1. All quotations are from F. Engels, "Socialism: Utopian and Scientific," in A. P. Mendel, ed., *Essential Works of Marxism* (New York: Bantam, 1961), pp. 70, 71, 77, 88.

2. See F. Engels, "Critique du programme d'Erfurt," in K. Marx and F. Engels, *Critiques des programmes de Gotha et d'Erfurt* (Criticisms of the programs of Gotha and Erfurt) (Paris: Editions Sociales, 1950), p. 83; and V. I. Lenin, "State and Revolution," in Mendel, *Essential Works of Marxism*, pp. 154-155.

3. See, for example, A. S. Gordon, *Sistema planovykh organov SSSR* (The system of planning organs of the USSR) (Moscow: Komakadizdat, 1929), passim.

4. Administrative management—i.e., executive leadership—involves, in a business corporation, planning and controlling the basic directions of its activities, its expansion, diversification, etc. Operational management involves the activities which result directly in salable products. Though overlapping, the two types of management and their respective functions tend to be differentiated in the great corporations.

5. Causality is assumed to contain an explanation of past events, a predictive element, and an interpretation of goal-directed phenomena (e.g., in biology, the development of the individual from the egg to the final stage of adult). In the discussion on Soviet planning, those who emphasized the role of objective regularities in economic change were called "geneticists" (from "genesis," origin, evolution). Those who, on the contrary, emphasized the role of the planner's purposive action were called "teleologists" (from "teleology," goal-directed development).

6. See S. Sharov, "Tsel' v plane i zadachi nashego khoziaistva" (The goal of the plan and the tasks of our economy), *Planovoe khoziaistvo* (1926), 7: 59-70.

7. S. G. Strumilin, "Perspektivnaia orientirovka na 1926/27-1930/-31" (Perspective guidelines for 1926/27-1930/31), Report to the Second Congress of Planning Agencies of the USSR, March 25, 1927, in

S. G. Strumilin, *Ocherki sovetskoi ekonomiki: Resursy i perspektivy* (Essays in Soviet economics: Resources and perspectives) (Moscow: Gosplanizdat, 1928), pp. 427 ff.

8. M. Ragolskii, "O vreditel'skoi teorii planirovania Gromana-Bazarova" (On the Groman-Bazarov subversive theory of planning), *Planovoe khoziaistvo* (1930), 10-11: 94.

9. Ragolskii writes that "balances" are to be "planned actively. . . . Balance is not manna falling from heaven, but the result of class struggle, initiative, and labor heroism." Ibid., p. 95.

10. See V. G. Groman, "O nekotorykh zakonomernostiakh . . ." (On certain regularities . . .), p. 89.

11. N. D. Kondrat'ev, "Kriticheskie zametki o plane razvitiia narodnogo khoziaistva" (Critical remarks on the plan of development of the national economy), *Planovoe khoziaistvo* (1927), 4: 1-34.

12. V. A. Bazarov, "O metodologii postroeniia perspektivnykh planov" (On the methodology of drawing up perspective plans), *Planovoe khoziaistvo* (1926), 7: 10.

13. Ibid., 11 ff.

14. V. G. Groman, "Balans narodnogo khoziaistva" (Balance of the national economy), *Planovoe khoziaistvo* (1926), 11: 62 ff.

15. N. I. Bukharin, *Zametki ekonomista k nachalu khoziaistvennogo goda* (Notes of an economist at the beginning of a new economic year) (Moscow-Leningrad: Gosizdat, 1928), p. 16.

16. S. G. Strumilin, "Perspektivnaia orientirovka na 1926/27-1930/-31" (Perspective guidelines for 1926/27-1930/31), pp. 423-424.

17. Ibid.

18. See S. G. Strumilin and G. M. Krzhizhanovskii, Introduction to Strumilin, ed., *Perspektivy razvertyvaniia narodnogo khoziaistva SSSR na 1926/27-1930/31* (Perspectives of development of the national economy of the USSR for 1926/27-1930/31), Materialy tsentral'noi komissii po piatiletnemu planu (Materials of the Central Commission on the Five-Year Plan) (Moscow: 1927), pp. 15-22.

19. N. D. Kondrat'ev, "Kriticheskie zametki . . ." (Critical remarks . . .), p. 9.

20. G. A. Fel'dman, "K teorii tempov narodnogo dokhoda" (On the theory of growth rates of national income), *Planovoe khoziaistvo* (1928), 12: 173.

21. N. A. Kovalevskii, "K postroeniiu general'nogo plana" (On the construction of the General Plan), with discussion, *Planovoe khoziaistvo* (1930), 3: 199-200.

22. See N. D. Kondrat'ev, "Kriticheskie zametki . . ." (Critical remarks . . .), pp. 5 ff.

23. N. I. Bukharin, *Zametki ekonomista* . . . (Notes of an economist . . .), p. 38.

24. M. Birbraer, "K voprosy o metodologii postroeniia 'perspektivnykh planov'" (On the methodological problem of constructing "perspective plans"), *Ekonomicheskoe obozrenie* (June 1927), p. 86. Fel'dman makes a similar remark in "K teorii tempov narodnogo dokhoda" (On the theory of growth rates of national income), p. 173.

25. M. Barengol'ts, "Emkost' promyshlennogo rynka v SSSR" (Capacity of the industrial market in the USSR), *Planovoe khoziaistvo* (1928) 7: 329.

26. For another type of experimentation with "chess board" balances see A. Boiarskii and L. Brand, "Problema statistiki tsen i tovarooborota" (The problem of statistics of prices and of trade turnover), *Planovoe khoziaistvo* (1930), 11: 239-277.

27. See above, pp. 40-44.

28. The type of baffling "unknown magnitudes" with which the Soviet planner had to deal and the ways in which he dealt with them are well illustrated by L. L. Lorwin and A. F. Hendricks in a study on Soviet planning in the 1930's. The example refers to a tractor factory: "What would be the ratable capacity under Russian conditions of maintenance? What would be the spoilage due to faulty raw materials or poor labor? How effective would raw peasants be in handling machinery—one tenth? one quarter? one half? two thirds as efficient as the American standard? How long would it take to train them? How rapidly would the efficiency of the individual advance? What would the average labor efficiency be; in other words, what rate of labor turnover would occur? No one can answer such questions with precision; but the answers will be pitched higher, if it is believed that the cooperation of the workers can be counted upon." See L. L. Lorwin and A. F. Hendricks, *National Economic and Social Planning* (Washington: National Planning Board, 1935), pp. 369-370 (mimeographed).

29. See above, p. 75; also p. 142, note 33.

30. A. S. Gordon, *Sistema planovykh organov SSSR* (The system of planning organs of the USSR), p. 26; also F. Pollock, *Die planwirtschaftlichen Versuche in der Sowjetunion 1917-1927* (Planning attempts in the Soviet Union 1917-1927) (Leipzig: C. L. Hirschfeld, 1929), pp. 111-112.

31. S. G. Strumilin, "Pervye opyty perspektivnogo planirovaniia"

(First experiences with perspective planning), *Planovoe khoziaistvo* (1930), no. 12; reprinted in S. G. Strumilin, *Na planovom fronte* (On the planning front) (Moscow: Gospolitizdat, 1958) pp. 274 ff. See also M. Markovich, "Itogi i perspektivy planovoi raboty" (Results and perspectives of planning work), *Sotsialisticheskoe khoziaistvo*, I (1924), 189 ff.

32. S. G. Strumilin, "Pervye opyty perspektivnogo planirovaniia" (First experiences with perspective planning), p. 274.

33. Osoboe soveshchanie po vosproizvodstvu osnovnogo kapitala, abbreviated to OSVOK.

34. These form the so-called "Piatakov Industrial Five-Year Plan." See *Materialy osobogo soveshchaniia po vosproizvodstvu osnovnogo kapitala pri Prezidiume VSNKh SSSR* (Materials of the Special Council on the Reproduction of Fixed Capital at the Presidium of the Supreme Council of the National Economy of the USSR): Series I, "Piatiletie gipotezy po otrasliam promyshlennosti" (Five-Year hypotheses by branches of industry) (Moscow-Leningrad: 1926); Series II, "Materialy k kritike gipotez" (Materials on the critique of the hypotheses) (Moscow-Leningrad: 1926); Series III, "Perspektivy razvitiia promyshlennosti na 1925/26-1929/30 (Perspectives for the development of industry for 1925/26-1929/30) (Moscow-Leningrad: 1927).

35. These "Materials" are sometimes designated as the "A. M. Ginzburg Five-Year Plan."

36. C. Bobrowski, *Formation du système soviétique de planification* (Formation of the Soviet planning system) (Paris and The Hague: Mouton, 1956), pp. 51 ff.

6. SOVIET "CORPORATE" PROCESSES AND PROBLEMS

1. K. Marx and F. Engels, *Critiques des programmes de Gotha et d'Erfurt* (Criticisms of the programs of Gotha and of Erfurt) (Paris: Editions Sociales, 1950), p. 82.

2. Ibid., p. 83.

3. N. I. Bukharin and E. A. Preobrazhenskii, *The ABC of Communism*, trans. by Eden and Cedar Paul for the Communist Party of Great Britain (London: Unwin Bros., 1922), p. 70. See also V. V. Obolensky-Ossinsky, *Social Economic Planning in the Union of Soviet Socialist Republics* (The Hague: International Industrial Relations, 1931), p. 27.

4. Gunnar Myrdal, "The Trend Toward Economic Planning," *Manchester School of Economic and Social Studies*, XIX (January 1951), 1: 3.

5. Ibid., p. 12.

6. Ibid., pp. 17 ff.

7. See E. S. Phelps, ed., *The Goal of Economic Growth* (New York: Norton, 1962), pp. vii ff., and Paul A. Samuelson, "Public Responsibility for Growth and Stability," ibid., pp. 38-42.

8. Let us recall here how Preobrazhenskii connects monopoly capitalism, monopoly prices, and Soviet "primary socialist accumulation": "Through the formation of monopoly prices . . . [monopoly capitalism] prepares the ground for the price policy of the period of primary socialist accumulation. The concentration of the whole of the big industry of the country in the hands of a single trust increases to an enormous extent the possibility of carrying out such a price policy on the basis of monopoly." E. A. Preobrazhenskii, *Novaia ekonomika* (New economics), Second Edition (Moscow: Komakadizdat, 1926), p. 123.

9. See Melville C. Branch, *The Corporate Planning Process* (New York: American Management Association, 1962), p. 72.

10. Ibid., p. 196.

11. "Much remains to be accomplished," writes Melville Branch, "in the development of a methodology of corporate planning. As yet there are few established procedures and techniques." Ibid., p. 33.

12. Such commitments arise notably "through debt, product selection, manufacturing methods, sales contracts, distribution system, industrial location, labor policy, employment contracts, or organization structure." Ibid., p. 109.

13. The fraction of the product invested, in real terms, has actually risen over time even if it has remained more or less constant in current prices.

14. See Edward A. Mason, *Economic Planning in Underdeveloped Areas* (New York: Fordham University Press), pp. 10 ff.

15. Dr. Jasny is correct when he assumes that Soviet planning methodology as practiced under Stalin was "largely developed before Stalin's men took over in 1927." But he is, I believe, in error when he assumes that crude balancing of resources and allocation around some priority branches is "basically the same thing" as input-output analysis. See Naum Jasny, *Essays on the Soviet Economy* (New York: Praeger, 1962), p. 161 and note 6, p. 162. This risks obscuring both the significance of present and impending changes in Soviet planning and the nature of the Sino-Soviet differences in this field.

Bibliography

1. GOALS AND INSTRUMENTS OF ECONOMIC DEVELOPMENT

Bukharin, N., and Preobrazhenskii, E., *The ABC of Communism* (1919), trans. by Eden and Cedar Paul for the Communist Party of Great Britain, London, Unwin Bros., 1922.

Carr, E. H., *A History of Soviet Russia: Socialism in One Country, 1924-1926*, vol. I, New York, Macmillan, 1958.

Daniels, R. V., *The Conscience of the Revolution: Communist Opposition in Soviet Russia*, Cambridge, Harvard University Press, 1960.

Erlich, A., *The Soviet Industrialization Debate, 1924-28*, Cambridge, Harvard University Press, 1960.

Higgins, B., *Economic Development: Problems, Principles and Policies*, New York, Norton, 1959.

Motylev, V. E., *Problema tempa razvitiia SSSR* (The problem of the pace of development of the USSR), Moscow, Komakadizdat, 1929.

Fhelps, E. S., ed., *The Goal of Economic Growth*, New York, Norton, 1962.

Preobrazhenskii, E. A., "Sotsialisticheskie i kommunisticheskie predstavleniia o sotsializme" (The Socialist and Communist images of socialism), *Vestnik kommunisticheskoi akademii* (Herald of the Communist Academy), no. 12, 1925, part I, pp. 19-75; no. 13, 1925, pp. 3-33.

————, *Novaia ekonomika: Opyt teoreticheskogo analiza sovet-skogo khoziaistva* (New economics: Attempt at a theoretical analysis of the Soviet economy), vol. I, part I, second enlarged edition, Moscow, Komakadizdat, 1926.

Savel'ev, M., *Direktivy VKP(b) v oblasti khoziaistvennoi politiki za 10 let, 1917-1927.* (Directives of the All-Union Communist Party [Bolsheviks] in the domain of economic policy for 10 years, 1917-1927), Moscow, Gosizdat, 1928.

Vsesoiuznaia Kommunisticheskaia Partiia (Bol'shevikov) v reso-liutsiiakh i resheniiakh S'ezdov, Konferentsii i Plenumov (All-Union Communist Party [Bolsheviks], resolutions and decisions of Congresses, Conferences and Plenums), part I, 1898-1924; part II, 1925-1939. Sixth edition, Moscow, Gospolitiz-dat, 1941, 1940.

2. THE SOVIET ECONOMY AND ECONOMIC LAWS

Akademiia Nauk (Academy of Sciences), *Politicheskaia eko-nomiia* (Political economy), Moscow, Gospolitizdat, 1954.

Bogdanov, A., *A Short Course of Economic Science*, second edition, London, Dorrit Press, 1927.

Bukharin, N., *Ekonomika perekhodnogo perioda: Obshchaia teo-riia transformatsionnogo protsessa* (Economics of the transition period: The general theory of the transformation process), part I, Moscow, Gosizdat, 1920.

Domar, E., "A Soviet Model of Growth," in *Essays in the Theory of Economic Growth*, New York, Oxford University Press, 1957.

Engels, F., "Socialism: Utopian and Scientific," in Mendel, A. P., ed., *Essential Works of Marxism*, New York, Bantam, 1961.

Fal'ker, S. A., "Iz istorii idei narodnokhoziaistvennogo balansa" (From the history of the idea of a national economic balance), *Planovoe khoziaistvo*, no. 10, 1928, pp. 153-174.

Fel'dman, G. A., "K teorii tempov narodnogo dokhoda" (On the theory of growth rates of national income), *Planovoe khozi-aistvo*, no. 11, 1928, pp. 146-171; no. 12, 1928, pp. 151-181.

Groman, V. G., "Balans narodnogo khoziaistva" (Balance of the national economy), *Planovoe khoziaistvo*, no. 11, 1926, pp. 62-80.

Heremberg, P., *Volkswirtschaftliche Bilanzen* (National Economic Balance), Leipzig, Akademische Verlagsgesellschaft, 1927.

Iurovskii, L. N., *Denezhnaia politika sovetskoi vlasti, 1917-1927* (The monetary policy of the Soviet government, 1917-1927), Moscow, Finansovoe Izd., 1928.

Jasny, N., "Soviet 'perspective' Planning," in *Essays on the Soviet Economy*, New York, Praeger, 1962.

Kaufman, A., "The Origin of the Political Economy of Socialism," *Soviet Studies*, January 1953, pp. 243-272.

Lange, O., *The Political Economy of Socialism*, Warsaw, Polish Institute of International Affairs, 1957 (mimeographed).

Lapidus, T., and Ostrovitsianov, K., *An Outline of Political Economy: Political Economy and Soviet Economics*, New York, International Publishers, 1930.

Lenin, V. I., *The Development of Capitalism in Russia* (1899), Moscow, Foreign Languages Publishing House, 1956.

———, "On the So-called Market Question" (1893), in *Collected Works*, Moscow, Foreign Languages Publishing House, 1960, vol. I, pp. 79-125.

———, "Zamechaniia na knigu N. I. Bukharina: 'Ekonomika perekhodnogo perioda'" (Comments on N. I. Bukharin's book "Economics of the transition period"), in Bukharin, N. I.; Molotov, V. M.; Savel'ev', A. U., eds., *Leninskii sbornik* (Lenin collection), vol. XI, Moscow, Gosizdat, 1929.

Leontief, W., "Balans narodnogo khoziaistva SSSR" (The balance of the national economy of the USSR), *Planovoe khoziaistvo*, no. 12, 1925, pp. 254-258.

———, "Significance of Marxian Economics for Present-Day Economic Theory," *American Economic Review*, supplement, 1938, 1: 1-9.

———, "The Decline and Rise of Soviet Economic Science," *Foreign Affairs*, January 1960, pp. 261-272.

Litoshenko, L., "Metodika sostavleniia narodno-khoziaistvennogo balansa" (Methods of constructing a national economic balance), in Popov, P. I., ed., *Balans narodnogo khoziaistva Soiuza SSR 1923/24 g.*, Trudy Tsentral'nogo Statisticheskogo Upravleniia, Tom XXIX (The balance of the national economy of the USSR, 1923/24. Transactions of the Central Statistical Office, vol. XXIX), Moscow, 1926.

Marx, K., *A Contribution to the Critique of Political Economy*, trans. by N. I. Stone, Chicago, Kerr and Co., 1911.

———, *Capital*, vol. II, Moscow, Foreign Languages Publishing House, 1957.

Marx, K., and Engels, F., *Critique des programmes de Gotha et d'Erfurt* (Criticisms of the Gotha and Erfurt Programs), Paris, Editions Sociales, 1950.

Mossé, E., *Marx et le problème de la croissance dans une économie capitaliste* (Marx and the problem of growth in a capitalist economy), Paris, Armand Colin, 1956.

Nemchinov, V. S., *Application of Statistical and Mathematical Methods in the Soviet Planning*, Report to the International Conference on Input-Output Analysis, Moscow, Academy of Sciences of the USSR, 1961.

Plekhanov., G. V., *The Materialist Conception of History*, London, Lawrence and Wishart, 1940.

Popov, P. I., "Balans narodnogo khoziaistva 1923/24" (Balance of the national economy in 1923/24), *Ekonomicheskaia zhizn'*, March 29, 1925.

———, ed., *Balans narodnogo khoziaistva Soiuza SSR 1923/24 g.*, Trudy Tsentral'nogo Statisticheskogo Upravleniia, Tom XXIX (The balance of the national economy 1923/24, Transactions of the Central Statistical Office, vol. XXIX), Moscow, 1926.

Preobrazhenskii, E. A., "Khoziaistvennoe ravnovesie v sisteme SSSR" (Economic equilibrium in the Soviet system), *Vestnik kommunisticheskoi akademii*, no. 22, 1927, pp. 19-71.

Shafiev, K. N., ed., *Politicheskaia ekonomiia sotsializma* (Political economy of socialism), Moscow, Sotsekgiz, 1960.

Spulber, N., *The Soviet Economy: Structure, Principles, Problems*, New York, Norton, 1962.

Stalin J. V., *Economic Problems of Socialism in the USSR*, New York, International Publishers, 1952.

Stepanov-Skvortsov, I. I., "Chto takoe politicheskaia ekonomiia" (What is political economy?) (Discussants: Bukharin, N.; Dvolaitskii, Sh. U.; Bogdanov, A. A.; Preobrazhenskii, E. A.; Ossinskii, V. V.; Pokrovskii, M. N.; Marestskii, D.; Kon, A. F.; Kritsman, L. N.; Smirnov, V. U.; and others), *Vestnik kommunisticheskoi akademii*, no. 11, 1925, pp. 257-346.

Sweezy, P. M., *The Theory of Capitalist Development: Principles of Marxian Political Economy*, New York, Oxford University Press, 1942.

Tinbergen, J., and Boz, H. C., *Mathematical Models of Economic Growth*, New York, McGraw-Hill, 1962.

Trotsky, L. D., *K sotsialismu ili k kapitalizmu? Analiz sovetskogo khoziaistva i tendentsii ego razvitiia* (Toward socialism or toward capitalism? Analysis of the Soviet economy and of the tendency of its development), Moscow-Leningrad, *Planovoe khoziaistvo*, 1925.

Wiles, P. J. D., *The Political Economy of Communism*, Cambridge, Harvard University Press, 1963.

3. STRATEGIES OF ECONOMIC DEVELOPMENT

Bazarov, V. A., "O metodologii postroeniia perspektivnykh planov" (On the methodology for drafting perspective plans), *Planovoe khoziaistvo*, no. 7, 1926, pp. 7-21.

————, "O nashikh khoziaistvennykh perspektivakh i perspektivnykh planakh" (On our economic perspectives and perspective plans), *Sotsialisticheskoe khoziaistvo*, no. 5, 1927, pp. 31-53.

————, "Printsipy postroeniia perspektivnogo plana" (Principles of constructing the perspective plan), *Planovoe khoziaistvo*, no. 2, 1928, pp. 38-64.

Bruton, H. J., "Growth Models and Underdeveloped Economies," *Journal of Political Economy*, August 1955, pp. 322-336.

Bukharin, N. I., *Nekotorye voprosy ekonomicheskoi politiki* (Some questions of economic policy), Moscow, Izd. TsUP'a VSNKh, 1925.

————, *Partiia i oppozitsionnyi blok* (The party and the opposition bloc), Leningrad, Priboi, 1926.

————, *K voprosu o zakonomernostiakh perioda: Kriticheskie zamechaniia na knigu E. Preobrazhenskogo "Novaia ekonomika"* (On the problem of regularities of the period: Critical remarks on the book of E. Preobrazhenskii: *New Economics*), Moscow-Leningrad, *Pravda*, 1926.

————, *Zametki ekonomista k nachalu novogo khoziaistvennogo goda* (Notes of an economist at the beginning of a new economic year), Moscow-Leningrad, Gosizdat, 1928.

Dobb, M., *Russian Economic Development since the Revolution*, New York, Dutton, 1928.

Erlich, A., *The Soviet Industrialization Debate, 1924-1928*, Cambridge, Harvard University Press, 1960.

Higgins, B., "Elements in a Theory of Underdevelopment," in Nelson, E., ed., *Economic Growth: Rationale, Problems, Cases*, Austin, University of Texas Press, 1960, pp. 32-68.

Hinkelammert, F. J., *Der Wachstumprozess in der Sowjetwirtschaft* (The Process of Growth in the Soviet Economy), Berlin, Duncker and Humblot, 1961.

Hirschman, A. O., *The Strategy of Economic Development*, New Haven, Yale University Press, 1958.

Katsenelenbaum, Z. S., *Industrializatsiia khoziaistva i zadachi kredita v SSSR* (The industrialization of the economy and the tasks of credits in the USSR), Moscow-Leningrad, Gosizdat, 1928.

Knirsch, P., *Die ökonomischen Anschauungen Nikolaj I. Bucharins* (The economic views of Nicholas I. Bukharin), Berlin, Duncker and Humblot, 1959.

Lenin, V. I., *The Development of Capitalism in Russia* (1899), Moscow, Foreign Languages Publishing House, 1956.

————, *Ob industrializatsii SSSR* (On the industrialization of the USSR), Moscow, Gosizdat, 1928.

Motylev, V. E., *Problema tempa razvitiia SSSR* (The problem of the pace of development of the USSR) Moscow, Komakadizdat, 1929.

"Platform of the Opposition," in L. D. Trotsky, *The Real Situation in Russia*, trans. by Max Eastman, New York, Harcourt, Brace, 1928.

Preobrazhenskii, E. A., *Novaia ekonomika: Opyt teoreticheskogo analiza sovetskogo khoziaistva* (New economics: Attempt at a theoretical analysis of the Soviet economy), second enlarged edition, Moscow, Komakadizdat, 1926.

————, "Ekonomicheskie zametki" (Economic notes), I, *Pravda*, December 15, 1925; II, *Bol'shevik*, no. 6, 1926, pp. 60-69; III, *Bol'shevik*, no. 15-16, 1926, pp. 69-83.

Scitovsky, T., "Two Concepts of External Economies," *Journal of Political Economy*, April 1954, pp. 143-151.

Shanin, L., "Ekonomicheskaia priroda nashego bestovar'ia" (The economic nature of our commodity shortage), *Ekonomicheskoe obozrenie*, no. 11, 1925, pp. 147-167.

————, "Voprosy ekonomicheskogo kursa" (Questions of the economic course), *Bol'shevik*, no. 2, 1926, pp. 65-87.

Singer, H. W., "The Concept of Balanced Growth in Economic Development: Theory and Practice," in Nelson, E., ed., *Economic Growth: Rationale, Problems, Cases*, Austin, University of Texas Press, 1960, pp. 71-86.

Stalin, J. V., "Industrialization and the Grain Problem" (1928), *Works*, Moscow, Foreign Languages Publishing House, 1954, vol. 11, pp. 165-196.

————, "Industrialization of the Country and the Right Deviation in the C.P.S.U.(b)" (1928), *Works*, cited, vol. 11, pp. 255-304.

————, "Concerning Questions of Agrarian Policy in the USSR" (1928), *Works*, cited, vol. 12, pp. 148-189.

Streeten, P., *Economic Integration: Aspects and Problems*, Leyden, Sythoff, 1961.

Strumilin, S. G., *Na khoziaistvennom fronte* (On the economic front), collection of articles (1921-25), Moscow-Leningrad, *Planovoe khoziaistvo*, 1925.

Trotsky, L., *The Third International after Lenin*, New York, Pioneer Publishers, 1957.

4. EFFICIENCY AND THE RATE OF GROWTH

Bazarov, V. A., *Kapitalisticheskie tsikly i vosstanovitel'nyi protsess khoziaistya SSSR* (Capitalist cycles and the restoration process of the Soviet economy), Moscow, Biblioteka po Voprosam Teoreticheskoi Ekonomiki, 1927.

Dobb, M., *An Essay on Economic Growth and Planning*, London, Routledge and Kegan Paul, 1960.

Fel'dman, G. A., "K teorii tempov narodnogo dokhoda" (On the theory of growth rates of national income), part II *Planovoe khoziaistvo*, no. 11, 1928, pp. 151-178.

————, "O limitakh industrializatsii (On the limits of industrialization), *Planovoe khoziaistvo*, no. 2, 1929, pp. 184-196.

Ginzburg, A. M., ed., *Materialy po izucheniiu effektivnosti kapitalovlozhenii v promyshlennosti* (Materials for the study of effectiveness of capital investments in industry), Moscow, Institut Promyshlennoekonomicheskikh Issledovanii of the VSNKh, 1928.

Grossman, G., "Suggestions for a Theory of Soviet Investment Planning," in *Investment Criteria and Economic Growth*, Cambridge, Center for International Studies, Massachusetts Institute of Technology, 1955 (mimeographed), pp. 89-115.

————, "Scarce Capital and Soviet Doctrine," *Quarterly Journal of Economics*, August 1953, pp. 311-343.

Materialy k piatiletnemu planu razvitiia promyshlennosti SSSR, 1927/28-1931/32 gg. (Materials for the Five-Year Plan of development of industry for the years 1927/28-1931/32), Moscow, Gostechnicheskoe Izd., 1927.

Motylev, V. E., *Problema tempa razvitiia SSSR* (The problem of the pace of development of the USSR), Moscow, Komakad-izdat, 1929.

Ragol'skii, M., "O vreditel'skoi teorii planirovaniia Gromana-Baz-arova" (On the Groman-Bazarov subversive theory of planning), *Planovoe khoziaistvo*, no. 10/11, 1930, pp. 59-97.

Sabsovich, L. M., *SSSR cherez 15 let: Gipoteza general'nogo plana, kak plana postroeniia sotsializma v SSSR* (The USSR in 15 years: Hypothesis of the General Plan, as a plan of the construction of socialism in the USSR), Moscow, *Planovoe khoziaistvo*, second edition, 1929.

Strumilin, S. G., "O tempakh nashego razvitiia" ("On the growth rates of our development), *Planovoe khoziaistvo*, no. 1, 1929, pp. 104-116.

5. PRINCIPLES AND PROCEDURES OF PLANNING

Bazarov, V. A., *K metodologii perspektivnogo planirovaniia* (The methodology of perspective planning), Moscow, Gosplan, 1924.

Bazhanov, B., "Kriticheskie zametki k kontrol'nym tsifram Gos-plana na 1925/26 g." (Critical remarks on the control figures of the Gosplan for the year 1925/26), *Sotsialisticheskoe kho-ziaistvo*, vol. 6, 1925, pp. 67-107.

Bobrowski C., *Formation du système soviétique de planification* (Formation of the Soviet planning system) Paris and The Hague, Mouton, 1956.

Dobb, M. H., "Economic Planning in the Soviet Union," *Science and Society*, Fall 1942.

Engels, F., "Critique du Programme d'Erfurt" (Criticism of the Erfurt Program), in Marx, K., and Engels, F., *Critiques des programmes de Gotha et d'Erfurt* (Criticisms of the Gotha and Erfurt programs), Paris, Editions Sociales, 1950.

Fal'ker, S. A., "Iz istorii idei narodnokhoziaistvennogo balansa" (From the history of the idea of a national economic balance), *Planovoe khoziaistvo*, no. 10, 1928, pp. 153-174.

Fel'dman, G. A. "Analiticheskii metod postroeniia perspektivnykh planov" (The analytical method of constructing perspective plans), *Planovoe khoziaistvo*, no. 12, 1929, pp. 95-127.

Gordon, A. S., *Sistema planovykh organov SSSR* (The system of
planning organs of the USSR), Moscow, Komakadizdat, 1929.

Jasny, N., "Soviet 'Perspective' Planning," in *Essays on the Soviet
Economy*, New York, Praeger, 1962.

Kaufman, A., "The Origin of the Political Economy of Socialism,"
Soviet Studies, January 1953, pp. 243-272.

Kondrat'ev, N. D., "Kriticheskie zametki o plane razvitiia narodnogo khoziaistva" (Critical remarks on the plan for the development of the national economy), *Planovoe khoziaistvo*, no. 4,
1927, pp. 1-34.

Kovalevskii, N. A., "Methodologiia plana rekonstruktsii narodnogo
khoziaistva SSSR" (Methodology of the plan of reconstruction
of the national economy of the USSR), *Planovoe khoziaistvo*,
no. 4, 1928, pp. 7-45.

―――, "K postroeniiu general'nogo plana" (On the construction
of the General Plan) (Discussants: Vaisberg, R. E.; Kon, A.;
Ragolskii, M.; Ioffe, P. V.; Mendel'son, L. A.; Rozentul, S.;
Eventov, L. Ia.; Koldovskii, I.; Fel'dman, G. A.; and others),
Planovoe khoziaistvo, no. 3, 1930, pp. 117-210.

Lange, O., *Essays on Economic Planning*, Calcutta, Indian Statistical Institute, Asia Publishing House, 1960.

Leontief, W., "The Decline and Rise of Soviet Economic Science," *Foreign Affairs*, January 1960, pp. 261-272.

Obolensky-Ossinsky, V. V., "The Nature and Form of Social Eco-
nomic Planning," in Obolensky-Ossinsky, V. V.; Ronin, S. L.;
Gayster, A.; Kraval, I. A., *Social Economic Planning in the
Union of Soviet Socialist Republics*, New York, Office of Vice-
President of Industrial Relations Association, 1931.

Pollock, F., *Die planwirtschaftlichen Versuche in der Sowjetunion
1917-1927* (Economic planning attempts in the Soviet Union
1917-1927), Leipzig, C. L. Hirschfeld, 1929.

Strumilin, S. G., "Perspektivnaia orientirovka Gosplana" (The
perspective orientational plan of Gosplan), *Planovoe khoziaistvo*, no. 4, 1926, pp. 31-58; no. 5, pp. 30-59.

————, *Industrializatsiia SSSR i epigony narodnichestva* (Industrialization of the USSR and the epigoni of the populist movement), Moscow-Leningrad, Gosizdat, 1927.

————, *Perspektivy razvertyvaniia narodnogo khoziaistva SSSR na 1926/27-1930/31 gg.* (Perspectives of the development of the national economy of the USSR for 1926/27 to 1930/31), Moscow, USSR Gosplan, 1927.

Tinbergen, J., *The Design of Development,* Baltimore, The Johns Hopkins University Press, 1958.

United Nations, "Economic Development and Planning in Asia and the Far East: Problems and Techniques," *Economic Bulletin for Asia and the Far East,* vol. VI, no. 3, 1955.

Zaleski, E., *Planification de la croissance et fluctuations économiques en U.R.S.S.* (Planning of growth and economic fluctuations in the USSR), vol. I, 1918-1932, Paris, Sedes, 1962.

6. SOVIET "CORPORATE" PROCESSES AND PROBLEMS

Branch, M. C., *The Corporate Planning Process,* New York, American Management Association, 1962.

Bukharin, N. I., and Preobrazhenskii, E. A., *The ABC of Communism* (1919), trans. by Eden and Cedar Paul for the Communist Party of Great Britain, London, Unwin Bros., 1922.

Jasny, N., *Essays on the Soviet Economy,* New York, Praeger, 1962.

Marx, K., and Engels, F., *Critiques des programmes de Gotha et d'Erfurt* (Criticisms of the Gotha and Erfurt Programs), Paris, Editions Sociales, 1950.

Mason, E. A., *Economic Planning in Underdeveloped Areas,* New York, Fordham University Press, 1958.

Myrdal, G., "The Trend toward Economic Planning," in *The Manchester School of Economic and Social Studies,* January 1951.

Phelps, E. A., *The Goal of Economic Growth,* New York, Norton, 1962.

Index

Abezgauz, G., criteria of efficiency, 92–93

agriculture: classical economic theory, 56–57; collectivization, 72, 73, 83, 85, 100; industry and, 8, 20, 100, 108; "kulaks," 24, 25, 69; Lenin's theory, 57–58; macro-economic models and, 45, 48, 52; Marxian theory, 57; planning and, 99, 100, 104, 107, 108, 114, 117; "scissors" crisis, 59–61; strategies of development, and industry, 59–74, 123–124, 125, 126, 127

allocation: factors, 116; intermediate products, 94; prices and, 36, 117; see also investment; resources

balances: "Balance of National Economy of USSR for 1923/24," 46–50; input-output analysis and, 47, 87, 103, 111; Marxian theory, 39–40; planning and, 103, 106, 108, 109–110, 111, 112; Soviet practice, 46, 49, 52, 116, 117, 118

banking, Soviet: debate on money in state sector, 36; nationalization, 24; see also money

Barengol'ts, M.: input-output analysis, 9, 52, 111, 118, 124; planning, 111

Barun, M., criteria of efficiency, 93

Bazarov, V. A.: fate under Stalin, 8; Menshevik trial, 86, 105; planning, 104, 126; rate of growth, 80; strategies of development, 71–72

Birbraer, M., planning, 110–111

Bogdanov, A. A.: "Bogdanovism," 51; economic laws of socialism, 31, 32, 34

Boiarskii, A., rate of growth, 81

Bolsheviks, see Communist Party of Soviet Union (CPSU)

branches of the economy: allocation among, 62, 83; balances and, 47, 48, 50, 108; differential growth rates, 98, 112, 125–126; planning and, 83, 98, 101, 102, 106-107, 108, 112, 113, 114, 116, 117, 122; strategies of development and, 20, 64–65, 72, 74, 83, 108, 112, 116, 117, 122, 124, 126, 127–128

Brazil, comparison with Soviet Union, 18, 21–23

Bukharin, N. I.: economics of socialism, 29–30, 31–32; fate un-